MW01634108

DISCLAIMER

This book reflects the personal views and beliefs of the author. In no way the author is endorsing the readers to follow his techniques and suggestions.

All the readers are suggested to evaluate their health and consult their doctors and financial consultants before acting on the advice given in this book.

Dedicated to my star – Iris

30 DAYS

CHALLENGE

LIVE THE MAGICAL LIFE

Authored by

DR. KUNAL BANKA

PENMAN BOOKS
A BOOK PUBLISHING COMPANY

PENMAN BOOKS

Office No. 303, Kumar House Building,
D Block, Central Market, Opp PVR Cinema,
Prashant Vihar, Delhi 110085, India
Website: www.penmanbooks.com
Email: publish@penmanbooks.com

First Published by Penman Books 2022
Copyright © Dr. Kunal Banka
All Rights Reserved.

Title: 30 Days Challenge
ISBN: 978-93-93651-46-4

No part of this book may be reproduced or transmitted in any form whatsoever, electronic, or mechanical, including photocopying recording, or by any informational storage or retrieval system without the expressed written, dated and signed permission from the author.

LIMITS OF LIABILITY/DISCLAIMER OF WARRANTY: The author and publisher of this book have used their best efforts in preparing this material. The author and publisher make no representation or warranties with respect to the accuracy, applicability or completeness of the contents. They disclaim any warranties (expressed or implied), or merchantability for any particular purpose. The author and publisher shall in no event be held liable for any loss or other damages, including but not limited to special, incidental, consequential, or other damages. The information presented in this publication is compiled from sources believed to be accurate, however, both the publisher and author assume no responsibility for errors or omissions. The information in this publication is not intended to replace or substitute professional advice. The strategies outlined in this book may not be suitable for every individual, and are not meant to provide individualized advice or recommendations.

The advice and strategies found within may not be suitable for every situation. This work is sold with the understanding that neither the author nor the publisher are held responsible for the results accrued from the advice in this book.

All disputes are subject to Delhi jurisdiction only.

CONTENTS

ABOUT THE AUTHOR ix

MAGICAL LIFE xi

HOW TO BEST USE THIS BOOK xiii

Chapter 1   The 30-Day Challenge 1

Chapter 2   Problems 7

Chapter 3   What do We Want from Life? 17

Chapter 4   Let's shatter the Myths 23

Chapter 5   Mind-Body-Soul 31

Chapter 6   Law of Attraction- A Power Greater Than
              Nuclear Power 39

Chapter 7   Brahma Muhurat- the Time for Treasure
              Hunt 45

Chapter 8   Meditate - Listen to Your Mind. 51

Chapter 9   Creative visualization 57

Chapter 10   Reading- Food for the Brain 65

Chapter 11   Exercise to a Champion Body 71

Chapter 12   Post Dinner Rituals 81

Chapter 13   The 8*3 Formula 85

Chapter 14   Manage Your Time like a Champion 91

Chapter 15   Relationships 97

Chapter 16   *Money Matters* 103
Chapter 17   *Money strategies.* 111
Chapter 18   *The Excuse Mindset* 117
Chapter 19   *Mind Map.* 123
Chapter 20   *Money Map* 125
Chapter 21   *Road Map.* 127

CONCLUSION **129**
SUGGESTED READS **131**
ACKNOWLEDGMENT **133**

"Many of life's failures are people
who did not realize how close they were
to success when they gave up."

—Thomas A. Edison

*"Everyone lives to survive...
but I want you to live,
to live your life KINGSIZE."*

—Dr. Kunal Banka

ABOUT THE AUTHOR

Dr. Kunal Banka is a dental surgeon by profession. He has been practicing dentistry in Ranchi, Jharkhand for 15 years. He is known for his expertise in implantology. He has been lecturing on dental implants all over the country.

Dr. Kunal embraces a vast experience in life and profession. He has made his place and name through rigorous hard work. Coming from a middle-class background, Dr. Kunal is always enthused to think out of the box, and this mindset has fetched him a boatload of accolades.

From nothing, he has risen to one of the most sought-after names in the field of dentistry. Besides, he has established himself as a magical life coach. Dr. Kunal has conducted numerous workshops for doctors as well as others on how to lead an amazing life.

MAGICAL LIFE

"The ultimate aim is a comfortable end
and a joyous road to it."
—Dr. Kunal Banka

Imagine you are bursting with health; you have an aerobicized body and perfect mental well-being. Happiness has always been your companion.

Financial worries are alien to you.

You have a loving spouse and affectionate children. You are cruising in one of the most exotic destinations in the world.

Financially and emotionally you are so well-shielded that your holidays are a part of your monthly calendar, staying in 5-star hotels and sipping your favorite cocktail.

How does this sound?

Now close your eyes and imagine yourself in the above scenario.

How do you feel?

Do you want this dream to be turned into a reality?

Well, go ahead and read this book. Read it over a weekend or whenever you are free, but try to finish it in one go. I have written it in a very simple language for a smooth reading experience.

However impossible it may look to live this dream, after reading this book, you will find yourself many steps closer to this MAGICAL life.

HOW TO BEST USE THIS BOOK

1. **Accountability Diary**: This book will be most useful when you are accountable to yourself. All the knowledge is of no use if you don't execute it.

   So, keep a diary thick enough to last for 30 days and record all the steps you take as mentioned in this book every day.

   This will help you get going every day and effectively.

2. I suggest that you **read the book in one go initially**. Don't do any exercises during the first read. Then, as you read for the second time, read it chapter-wise and do each exercise as mentioned. This will yield you maximum benefit.

3. **Commitment**: I need a commitment from you that you will read the complete book and follow the steps for 30 days. These can be the life-changing 30 days for you.

   Happy Reading!

CHAPTER ONE

THE 30-DAY CHALLENGE

"Only those who will risk going too far can possibly find out how far one can go."
—T. S. Eliot

The period of the globe-trotting pandemic has been the biggest transition of the 21st century so far. During this time, many words and phrases that remained dormant in the vocabulary, all of a sudden, came to life, like the new normal, social distancing, sanitization, quarantine, lockdown, containment zone, WFH (work from home), etc. It was also the phase that witnessed numerous loss of lives and layoffs. Stress and insecurity were something that hula-hooped on almost every home on the street.

However, those two years of covid have been the best years of my life!

You must be wondering, have I gone mad?

No, these two years have transformed my life. Yes, I had no money, no resources, and my future looked bleak.

I was under tonnes of loans. I found myself like a spinning wheel stuck in the mud. Does this ring a bell? Can you relate to any of your life incidents where you found yourself in the same position? Or maybe in covid times? My only source of income, my clinic, was closed due to covid. I would spend nights wondering what will be the future. How will I survive? The worst part was that I did not want to share this with my wife and family members. Why burden them unnecessarily?

Every morning, I woke up with a heavy heart, wondering which creditor will ask for money!

All my aspirations were gone for a toss. I felt worthless, like an unnecessary piece of God's creation.

Then the magic happened. One fine day, I was lying on the bed, staring at the ceiling, wondering about my future. Suddenly, I realized that instead of being so disappointed, I should be thankful that I have a roof above my head and I have three meals on the table for me and my family!

And this changed my life forever. For the first time, I felt gratitude for what I had. And this gratefulness never died again. Gradually, one good thing led to another, and my life changed.

So, I decided not to limit the triggers of change to myself. Therefore, in this book, I have shared how things worked for me and what worked for me. This book guides you to a well-designed plan to make your dreams come true and your life magical. Interestingly, all these changes can be brought about in just 30 days.

This book is based on what I have learned over years from the greats of life, by reading a lot of wonderful books and implementing all that in my life.

When the results started showing up, I felt an urgency to spread the word around so that others can benefit from my experiences.

Let me start from the beginning so that you know the full story. It's a long journey, but I will try to condense it in this one chapter.

However, I promise you that my long story will be a part of my next book.

2001

This was the year when my story began. Although it began in 1983, December, when I was born. But I will keep it for some other time.

After prolonged struggle and persuasion by my parents, I took admission in a dental school in 2001. I had left my engineering seat and joined the dental college.

In the initial year, I understood that I had chosen a wrong profession. None of my natural inclinations were toward medical science.

Still, I had no option. I was from the family of an honest government officer. That itself ensured that there was never plenty of money in our home.

I had pledged to myself that I will do something in life so that I never have to face such a crisis of money. I told my father that I was not there to be a dentist… but to be the best dentist in the country!

I had to do it even if I had no interest in the subject. There was no choice.

Five years passed with a lot of difficulty in the subject. Somehow, I managed to clear my exams and get the degree. But the road to the degree was full of missed lunches so that I could eat at night.

I guess, by now, you know my background well.

After graduating, I started my practice by taking a loan for my clinic setup. I chose not to do my post-graduate studies as I had no money for higher studies. I had to earn money at a very rapid rate.

Those were very tough years, but I sailed through. There were days and months when I dint have a patient in my clinic.

But I was determined to move ahead with grit and persistence. I never gave up.

And it paid off well.

In a very few years, I became a famous doctor. My practice filled up fast and I got national fame in the dental circuit.

However, that was not enough for me to feel accomplished. I had promised my father that I would be the best dentist in the country. Meanwhile, in the madness to become top-notch, I forgot the promise I had made to myself that I will never see the lack of money again. I became careless on the financial front.

I kept soaring like a growth fuelled by steroids. At the same time, I took loans for expensive equipment. These loans amounted to more than 1 crore. This was against all the advice I had got. I always trusted my instincts.

But my instincts or even Nostradamus himself could not exactly foretell when covid would strike.

Covid stuck and stuck hard, it took me down hard. It hurt so bad that when I recovered from the fall, I decided that I will never ever again make the same mistakes.

I learned from my mistakes and had my lessons for a lifetime.

It was during covid when I made my gritty comeback. I always felt that I have a fighter inside me, but probably it was on snooze mode. However, during that challenging phase, I saw that fighter for the first time. This fighter came, saw, and conquered everything it got to.

Yes, that's what I did.

Here is a list of things I did:

1. I worked on my mindset and became an undefeatable warrior.

2. I worked on my patient base and got all my clients back with a lot of innovation. I had to think out of the box and work out of the box.

3. I improved and solidified my finances.

4. I worked relentlessly on my health, as I knew that only mental and physical fitness can make me invincible.

5. I turned a deaf ear to the syndrome "what people would say?" Sometimes, I feel it's the biggest disease of the modern day.

6. I started living in the moment.

This book is a compilation of my learnings and I will feel privileged if I could help at least a few of my fellow countrymen.

I give you the challenge to change your life in 30 days by following the steps explained in this book… here comes the 30-day challenge!

> *If you don't give up, you still have a chance.*
> *Giving up is the greatest failure.*
>
> **—Jack Ma**

CHAPTER TWO
PROBLEMS

"We cannot solve our problems with the same thinking we used when we created them."
—Albert Einstein

WHAT IS LIFE?

WHAT IS MORE IN LIFE? MISERY OR ABUNDANCE?

WHY IS IT THAT WE HUMAN BEINGS ARE ALWAYS SURROUNDED BY PROBLEMS?

I kept asking these questions to everyone for a long time. Every morning after I woke up, I found my mind being a launchpad to such questions with no answers.

After prolonged spells of thinking and suffering, I discovered this world is a merry place, and each one of us has access to abundance. It's just that we don't see it.

We are so driven by our limiting mindsets that we don't see what's there in this universe waiting for us.

Let me summarize the problems we, as human beings, have been facing in this modern era.

These challenges are related to the three most important pillars of life: PHYSICAL HEALTH, MENTAL HEALTH and MONEY.

PHYSICAL HEALTH

- HIGH BP
- Obesity
- Early diabetes
- Heart problems in the late 30s
- Lethargy
- Poor body form
- Unfit routine
- Unable to take part in sports
- Eyesight problems
- Lack of sleep (insomnia)

MENTAL HEALTH

- Irritability
- Depression
- Lack of interest in life
- No creativity
- No purpose in life
- Difficulty in concentration
- Frequent headaches

- Stress
- Always bored
- No motivation
- Habit to scheme, gossip and lie
- Bad relationships
- Low self-esteem

FINANCE

- No financial planning
- No financial security
- No financial goal
- Living pay-cheque-to-pay-cheque
- Always in the need of money
- Not prepared for emergencies
- Always asking others for money
- Poor money mindset

These are some common problems most of us face at some or other point in our lives. I am sure you resonate with some or most of these problems listed above.

We are so entangled in this web of problems that we never have the time to look beyond these and grow in our lives.

From the lens of my experience, I can tell you it's not so difficult to get this pile of problems out of our lives.

I was stuck in these problems for long 37 years of my life. I always wanted to live a magical life that is free of these problems, but I never knew how to break loose.

I am sure, by now, you might have gathered what a magical life is; i.e., a life free of the tight spots listed above.

However, before we make our headway to the solutions, let us first understand how we get into this trap of life. I believe none of us wants to be entangled in this cobweb of life. But life keeps luring us to such rabbit holes and we keep falling for them until one fine day we realize that it's too late!

PHYSICAL HEALTH

I hope you have heard the old saying 'health is wealth'.

Have you ever wondered why some wise man ever said that?

Well, it's simple… if we are healthy, only then we can make efforts to become wealthy. And when we are sick, no amount of wealth can compensate for our good health. So, health is wealth.

Now consider this… we all were born with almost the same health. Then why does it happen that as we grow up, some are athletic, some are obese, some are fat, skinny, some are smart and some are slow?

If we leave aside the genetic considerations which account for a very small percentage of health qualities, what is the reason that the health score varies for each one of us?

It is because of the environment in which we grow, the people around us, the choice we make in life and the mental toughness or GRIT (as mentioned by Angela Duckworth).

Choices form an important aspect at every step of our life. The same is true in the domain of our health. Our bodies have a high metabolism till our early 20s, so we don't see much effect of bad habits till that time. But as the body starts aging, that is, when we reach our 30s, the same bad habits start to backfire. It doesn't happen overnight. We laid the foundation for it in our teens by not eating healthy and not exercising.

These days, the screen-time of our kids is quite extensive. It leads to bad eyesight and poor mental health. Lack of focus is one of the main results of high screen-time.

Heart attacks in the early 30s and 40s are a result of the daily lifestyle and its spreading like a pandemic.

We tend to skip exercise by giving the excuse that 1) I don't have time due to my busy work schedule 2) I don't need to exercise, I look fit.

If you are one of those people who relay such reasons, then, my friend, be alert… you are inviting high BP, heart attack or diabetes.

We all need a minimum of 30 minutes of heavy exercise 5 days a week from an early age.

Those who don't exercise invite many diseases into their lives and, at the same time, reduce their life expectancy by a minimum of 7 years.

Consider the cost of it. Being afflicted with diseases means increased medical bills which leak out our finances and we know very well that these expenses can be avoided.

Additionally, you attract a restricted lifestyle. Don't eat this, don't eat that! This shrinks the joy of life.

I prefer eating everything throughout my life in controlled portions, rather than munching uncontrollably for a few years and then not eating some foods at all!

Our eating habits are another aspect of health. These days, we have lots of social gatherings, eat-outs, parties and official gatherings. What do we eat there? Mouth-watering cuisines. But have you ever thought about what that food does to your body?

Let me tell you. This greasy and fried food clogs your blood vessels with fat. This can translate into diseases like BP, high cholesterol, and may cause a heart attack. Now think this is the cost of exposing the body to bad stuff.

So you are the reason for your bad health.

What's the solution? Moderation is the key. When I receive a social invitation, I have my dinner at home and then go to the party. I don't feast on anything which can cause a disease to me and turn me pale. Even if I have to, I take a very small portion. I also make it a point to come back home in time so that the next morning, I can wake up on time for my exercise.

MENTAL HEALTH

Mental health is one of the most important aspects of life which is often ignored. A majority of us think we are fine.

But the reality is that most of us have some or other mental health issues. Mental health is not always related to madness. It has a bigger meaning.

A person taking a lot of stress is also suffering from mental health issues. And someone feeling lonely or depressed is a mental issue as well.

These days, irritability and short temper have also become very common. Lack of focus is very common among youngsters who are always hooked to their phones or computer screens.

What causes this? It's only and only our lifestyle. We don't realize but our habits have put us in a downward spiral of bad mental health.

When was the last time you spent a full day with your family when you were completely uninterrupted by your phone?

Most of the time, we have our teeth sunk into the phone and then we long for the goodness of life we are missing on.

Our overloaded work schedule, bad priority setting, too much competition at work, ambitions, habit to neglect family and self, and not valuing our relationships are a few reasons for our poor mental health.

We have to consciously avoid these traps and aspire for real success in life which holds a lot of happiness for us. At the same time, we must realize the importance of 'me time'. Nurturing self is very important, as this empowers us to spread happiness to others.

Our mental health is in our hands. We just have to set our priorities right. I have explained this in the chapter The 8*3 Formula and have shared a step-by-step guide on how to focus on improving our mental health.

Meditation is one of the ways to keep this in check. At the end of the chapter shared above, I have mentioned an exercise. After doing that exercise, I am sure you will know the right way of magical life.

FINANCE

How often do you feel that your salary gets exhausted before the month ends? Or that you never have enough money, whatever raise you get?

This is the story of a majority of people, whether salaried or self-employed.

Even I was in the same boat a few years ago. I was growing my practice at a fast pace, but I never had enough money whenever I needed it. And money is our best friend. But I did not know how to manage my money.

My expenses were uncontrolled, and as I was earning, I was spending recklessly. So my earnings never made me rich.

On the other hand, if your expenses are equivalent to your income, even this will never make you wealthy. It will just give you a momentary lifestyle high.

I learned it the tough way when my income dried during covid. It was a tough phase, but it gave me a new perspective.

As things got better and I started generating some revenue in my practice, I started cutting down my expenses to the level that my income became considerably higher than my expenses. I sliced off all the unnecessary expenses.

Very soon I could see money in my account. And then I came to know the concept of an emergency fund. I generated it in very little time as my monthly expenses became less.

It split-opened the gates to the peace of mind that I have been enjoying after my financial ramp-up.

This is not just my story. Most of us make the same mistakes. But we don't realize it until we are deep in trouble.

In this book, I have given a deep perspective on money. In the end, I have shared a money map. It will help you in your financial planning and securing your future.

CHAPTER THREE

WHAT DO WE WANT FROM LIFE?

"The purpose of our lives is to be happy."
—Dalai Lama

Every person on this planet is born for a purpose.

And this purpose is to live a life of abundance. To enjoy the richness of this universe and be good to our surroundings.

But what we do to our lives… most of us are eyeball-to-eyeball with lots of problems and stress. We are constantly worried about money, career, survival, loans, developing our business/careers and relationships, and many of us are struggling to sort these out. The harder we try to resolve our issues, the more we get submerged in the quicksand. Living our dream life, therefore, becomes like a mirage. Have you ever wondered who puts us in whatever good, bad or ugly situations we are in?

The answer is a big 'WE'.

Yes, you have read it right; it is only us who are responsible.

What do we all want in our lives - money, peace and relationships and success? If we are able to accomplish these four attributes, our life is like a heaven, else a hell, with the never-ending mirage chase.

All of us work towards attaining these, but very few go about it in the right way. We follow the wrong path and don't understand gratitude and the law of attraction. Attaining a good quality of life involves the well-being of our---MIND----BODY----SOUL.

If we nurture these three things, then we can all achieve:

MONEY---PEACE---RELATIONSHIPS---SUCCESS

The moment we realize that the purpose of our life is to enjoy riches, our perspective changes and we start looking at life through new, refined glasses.

The day I was awakened to this, the world changed for me. My priorities and purpose in life changed.

There is a systematic approach to changing our paths and reaching prosperity. It's only that we have to understand the law of attraction and gratitude. Being grateful helps us to nurture our soul and send positive signals to the universe. It works like magic. If you understand these two mechanisms, you will be able to fulfill all your wishes magically.

Always remember that money comes only after success. So we should first focus on becoming successful.

I have written separate chapters on the law of attraction and gratitude to give you more clarity on these two basic concepts so that you can make the maximum out of this book.

I have also shared a set of exercises to be done over a period of 30 days. If you do these exercises honestly, which I believe you will, you will realize that there was an unexplored part of the universe that was yours, but you were not aware of it. It will lead to the doorway of endless opportunities.

There is an ancient saying:

ASK AND IT SHALL BE GIVEN

SEEK AND YOU SHALL FIND IT

KNOCK AND IT SHALL BE OPENED

Write these lines on a piece of paper and place it at a place on your desk where you can see it many times a day.

You have to believe in this without doubt and it will come true. A slightest hint of doubt will make it less effective.

There are numerous people in this world, including me, who have transformed their lives and entered a world of plenty, leaving behind a life of misery.

Misery ends the moment we are clear about our goals in life. So, I would like you to make your dreams list immediately. It can be anything and in any number. Even if it's absurd, no problems. Make a list of as many dreams as possible and keep it to yourself.

Writing them is a must. Just thinking about it won't do. When we write anything, we send a very strong message to the universe to make our wishes come true.

So here comes our first **exercise**:

Make two lists:

LIST 1

Write all your dreams; be it your dream of owning a big house, a big car, any career goal, health goals, or any possible dreams you might want to achieve in the long term.

Make separate sections like: career, money, business, health, relations, personal ambitions/desires. Under each heading, write your dream as if you are already living it. For example, if you want to own a big house with a swimming pool, you can write it as: I am having a very nice big house with a swimming pool. I love my house and I am thankful to the universe for my house.

Then take at least a minute and imagine yourself living in that house, and notice how you feel.

Repeat this for every dream of yours.

Start your sentence with 'I am' and finish with gratitude towards the universe.

This method is one of the gifts to us from Rhonda Byrne's works.

LIST 2

Make a list of your short-term goals that you aim to achieve in the next 3-6 months. Follow the same steps as mentioned previously, visualize your goal and live it for a minimum of one minute.

Now keep your dream lists in a place where you can see them every day. Read these once every day, either at bedtime or first thing in the morning when you wake up.

"Life is what happens when you're
busy making other plans."

—John Lennon

CHAPTER FOUR

LET'S SHATTER THE MYTHS

Have you ever wondered why very few people in this world are very successful while others live a mediocre life and the rest are always struggling?

This is because of our average mentality, which has been programmed in us for ages. We are told that we have to lead an average life, and this is the only pathway to success.

The real meaning of success is hidden from us for some strange, unknown reasons.

In the modern world, we are taught that first; we have to study and attain a degree, get married, have children and then keep on living an average life. We have to obtain a house, some bank balance and that's enough to be good in this society.

The best example of herd mentality is our modern society, where we follow a set of average rules and mimic each other by following such average ideas.

What's the reason for such an attraction toward mediocre life? It is the myths of our society that are taught to us from our childhood by our parents and grandparents who were also taught the same values by their elders.

We have to break these myths and come out of them to reach a magical life.

Have you ever thought what if Thomas Alva Edison had chosen to remain mediocre and not thought of something new? What would have happened to our lives without a bulb?

What if the Wright brothers had not thought out of the box? Airplanes would have been something extra-terrestrial to us!

Human history is full of examples of great people who thought the unthinkable and dared to venture beyond the social norms. The result was great inventions which make our life so easy these days.

All these inventions were first created in the mind of our great scientists and then they materialized. They dared to break out of social mediocrity.

However, to shatter these myths and to rise above average, we need to first be aware of our limiting thoughts.

MONEY IS BAD.... IS IT?

We should not run after money. Money is the source of all evil.... don't do this... don't do that... don't think too much about material possessions... and so on. Such beliefs have been imbibed in our minds for ages by our parents, our parents' parents and so on. But have you ever wondered what this thought process does to you? It pushes you even deeper into the zone of negativity.

And we get what we believe in! So, if we believe that money is bad… we won't get it. If we believe we should not go after comforts and worldly pleasures, then the universe robs us of them. And we end up complaining that we don't have this and that, we don't become successful and always think about the lacks in our life.

Let's say, you go out for shopping and you like a pair of expensive shoes. But then you think… these shoes are too pricey and you can't afford them. This thought process creates a feeling of scantiness and attracts scarcity from the universe. The result is that we never are able to buy that pair of shoes. (example taken from The Secret)

The right way to think would be that these shoes are nice and very soon I am going to buy them. Once you have this mindset, the whole universe conspires to get those shoes to you. Not only in the case of shoes, but in all other fields of life. This is how the way of thinking separates the average from the best, failures from success!

We always have to have the feeling of plenty and that can be only attained by being in gratitude. Here, I suggest that you read the book The Magic by Rhonda Byrne. In this book, she has taught us very well how to stay in gratitude.

Once we and our whole existence are deep in gratitude, our path to success becomes very clear and well defined. In fact, we start seeing all the new opportunities on our way.

I agree that money is not everything. But the fact in life is that money is the source of all happiness.

ASKING IS BAD???

From our childhood, we have been taught that we should not ask others for what we want. We have always been told to make sacrifices for other family members. But have you ever noticed, there were other kids around us who took what they wanted by asking? They got everything, be it their favorite ice cream or being friends with the person of their choice. They were not timid, thus they enjoyed their life. There was never a lack around them. The same thing holds true in our life.

We should ask the supreme power/universe, for whatever we want, just like we asked our parents when we were kids. And just like a loving parent, the universe fulfills our wishes. We only have to ask! Isn't it simple…

But from ages, we have been taught that we should be satisfied with what we have and we should not be greedy. But all successful people have become successful only by breaking the shackles created in their brains by modern ancient wisdom. We should, from now on, believe and follow these three steps for realizing all our dreams:

1. ASK

2. BELIEVE

3. RECEIVE

These three steps are scientifically proven and are the holy grail of success. If these mental steps are executed well, they can change the world for you, as it has done for many successful people.

Whatever we want, first we have to ask it in our minds. We must see it in our minds.

WE CAN HOLD WHATEVER WE CAN THINK

Once we are focussed on what we want and we are very clear about it, we ask the universe to give it. And the universe, like a caring parent, will give it to us.

To receive gifts from the universe, we have to believe that we are going to get what we want in our due time. Once our belief is strong, only then we will get what we desire.

Imagine… if we don't ask, how will the supreme parent- the universe know what we need?

It's the same as we try to understand what our kids want, but we know it perfectly only when they ask for it.

So how can asking be bad? You have to ask and ask in the right places to get what you want and what you deserve.

Here, I am not at all implying that we will get whatever we want only by asking, sitting in our houses. No. even in a restaurant, we get our desired food only when we go there.

So we have to set our goals and demands to the universe and then work towards it. Remember, nothing can be achieved without working towards it. KARMA!

ACTION is the supreme necessity for a result.

There are so many people who work hard, but they don't know what they want. On the other hand, there are people who know what they want but they refuse to work towards it.

Both these types are failures, always living that mediocre life.

The right way is:

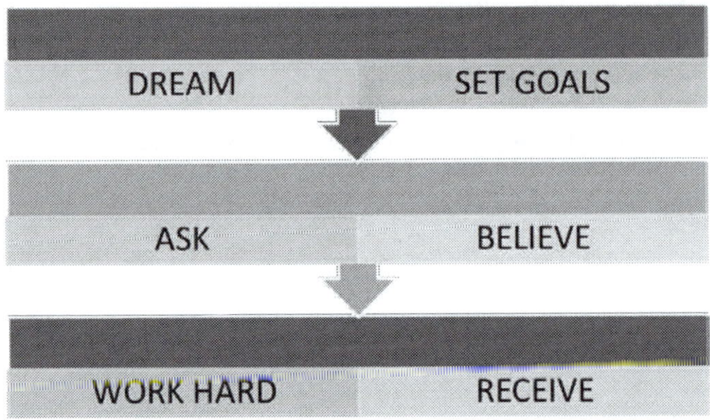

I have always believed in smart plus hard work. But the day I realized the importance of asking, and I learned the art of communicating with the universe, everything changed for me.

Things became easier, efforts started paying off.

Goals became achievable and life lovable.

Before I got this wisdom, I would easily be disheartened by the difficulties of life. During my lean phase, when life looked dark, I did not stop working towards that magical life that I wanted for myself.

I kept on working hard and found a new way of life which has now become the way of my life.

In this book, I have integrated the gems of life, which I learned through my struggle, and have put them in a way that you can use to make your life magical.

EXERCISE

1. Make a list of all your limiting beliefs you can think of and be honest with yourself.

2. Write in front of your beliefs how they have stopped you from growing.

3. Make another list of your new beliefs and thought process.

4. Now burn the first list as a symbol of burning your old limiting beliefs.

5. Read the list of your new beliefs every day for the next 30 days.

CHAPTER FIVE

MIND-BODY-SOUL

"What the mind dwells upon, the body acts upon."
—Denis Waitley

If we understand that the whole universe is energy, then we can easily surmise that our mind-body-soul and all physical possessions, including money, are a form of energy. We all know that energy can be channelized. Our mind is the apparatus, we must channelize, utilize, transmit and receive all forms of energy.

Imagine a large pool of energy which is the universe and a small segment of it as our mind-body-soul. This is how every human is aligned with this universe. It also means that we are a part of the universe and the universe is our part.

This simply explains the giving nature of our universe. We can harness any amount of unlimited energy from this huge source of energy if we ask for it in the right way. If we ask for it in the wrong way, then of course we get bad things in our life.

To channelize this energy in the right direction, we need to have a very good flow of energy between our mind, body and soul.

Our mind and body are interdependent, and the soul feeds on the mind.

To understand this, imagine a man who is very sick and is in the bed for… say, a month. Will he have a healthy mind? Will he think about the next holiday he will be taking? Or will he think about going for a picnic? Most of us won't have any happy thoughts in this situation. Thus, a sick body makes our mind sicker.

On the other hand, let's take the example of a person who is fit but constantly harbors sad thoughts. He often ponders over his bad experiences of the past and what adversities could happen to him in the future. Gradually, his body might start showing signs of disease and aging. Therefore, he may need to consult a doctor. This could cure him, but temporarily. He will never be happy.

Now, in the first scenario, if that man is strong-willed, and he understands the law of attraction, he will thank the universe that he is still alive and will plan to meet his family after getting well. Such people, who are thankful and constantly think about what they want, recover very soon. There are numerous examples in the history of medical science where the doctors gave up but the sheer gratitude and law of attraction have done miracles to the patients' health.

In the second case, if the person in question starts exercising, nourishing his body and accepting positivity in his present, his mental state will improve dramatically.

This means that we can control both our body and mind harmoniously. If these are in good health, then our soul is nourished, and this takes our existence to a whole new level.

How to keep our mind, body and soul in fine fettle and well-synchronized?

How to transmit that energy from our brain to the universe which sends the right messages?

Well, here is the answer and the routine which will change your life forever and for good. Let's see how we can do it.

MIND:

We need to be grateful to have a healthy mind.

1. Before you go to bed, think about the events of the day and the best thing that happened to you that day. Take a minute and say in your mind 'thank you for.......................as it helped me .... (mention the reason how that event helped you)'. Be in a state of gratitude for at least one minute. It will feel so good that you would like to stay in that state for a very long time.

   When we think happy thoughts at bedtime, it sets the tone for our mind to be happy subconsciously when we are sleeping. This sends a very positive signal to the universe, which gives us equally good things in return.

2. When you wake up in the morning, always start your day with gratitude, as has been advocated by many successful people.

Starting your day with gratitude sets your day up very nicely to face the challenges of the day. The hormones released in your body when you are in gratitude do wonders to your physical and mental health.

A gratitude practice can be done by writing 5 things you are grateful for on that day. You can also feel gratitude for your body parts. I do this very often. I thank each of my body parts for their function. It just takes 5 minutes but makes a lot of difference in your life.

You can also write gratitude for your loved ones like your spouse, children, parents and friends.

Another aspect of mental health is organizing and prioritizing.

Take 5 mins to make a to-do list for the day and mark the top 3 tasks of the day which are most important.

Take time for meditating, even if you think this stuff is not for you or you are not made for it. You can meditate even for 10 minutes and believe me; you will love it.

Remember, magic happens in the morning hours. If you want to achieve a magical life, you will have to invest some time in the morning before everyone else wakes up. Initially, it could be difficult, but gradually you will find it very easy and useful.

I have written in great details about meditation in a separate chapter Meditate.

BODY

Remember:

1. Our body is a place of worship

2. We are what we eat

3. We should take care of our body like it's the most prized possession we have

The most valuable and sophisticated machine God has given us is our body. Still, most of us don't know the importance of our body. Caring for our body comes last on our agenda. WHY?

We ignore our body because we take it for granted. We never paid any money to the nature for creating our body. Thus, we don't value it.

Let's say Mr. Ignorant is an entrepreneur. He has lots of money, more than he can spend in one lifetime. He is very proud of it and very happy about his money.

But Mr. Ignorant never takes care of his body. He never exercises. He is suffering from all sorts of lifestyle diseases and he can't take up a sport due to his weight and poor heart. He can't eat his favorite sweets as he has high blood sugar levels!

How will you rate his life? Or would you like to step into his body as he is very rich and has all worldly possessions?

I am sure none of us would like to be like him. But have we ever thought about what are we doing to our lives? In pursuit of success and money, we are following our industrialist friends' life. We ignore our body at every step. We avoid exercise just to give more time to work or maybe we are lazy.

But what are we doing to ourselves? We are slowly but surely spoiling and degenerating our most expensive possession- our body.

It is valuable because no money can buy you a new body for yourself!

Money can only repair our body to some limited extent. But once spoiled, we can never get our body back.

So friends, wake up and rise. Give it all. Embrace your body with the respect and care it deserves.

Start exercising at least for 30 minutes a day, start eating mindfully and make the right food choices. Make it a part of your daily life. One improvement at a time.

You won't get miraculous results in one day or a month, but slowly you will enter that area where you can call yourself fit. Make health a daily habit to unveil a new yourself.

Start by doing what I have explained for the next 30 days and after that, notice how you feel. All of my mentees have chosen to continue this regime even after a month and most of them have transformed into living a magical life.

SOUL

Once our mind and body are fit, then our soul starts to feel nourished. But the fitness of the soul comes from contentment.

Every day, we do so much for our profession, loved ones, friends and many more. But how many times do you pause in your day, maybe for 5 minutes or more, to do something for yourself?

Probably, enjoying your favorite coffee or reading a few pages or playing a game or listening to your favorite music or shopping for yourself or going for a walk alone.

The above examples are perfect indulgences for our me-time. This me-time is very much necessary for our soul even if we don't realize it.

Once upon a time, I was too busy in my profession and never took any me-time. I was successful, but not happy. My soul was not nourished.

The day I hit upon the significance of me-time, my life changed. You will have to take time out of your schedule to do something for yourself. This is compulsory, as without this, your soul will always be undernourished.

"I certainly believe that being in contact with one's spirit and nurturing one's spirit is as important as nurturing one's body and mind."
—Laurence Fishburne

EXERCISE

1. For the next 30 days, take out time to do something for yourself. Note down at the end of the day, what activity you did for yourself and how did you feel after that.

2. Make an exercise schedule for the next 30 days. Work out in some form and make a diary entry for that. Next to it, mention how you feel.

3. Meditate daily for the next 30 days. Note down what thoughts were coming to your mind during the practice. And you will be amazed to read your thoughts.

CHAPTER SIX

LAW OF ATTRACTION- A POWER GREATER THAN NUCLEAR POWER

"Everything you want is out there waiting for you to ask. Everything you want also wants you. But you have to take action to get it."
—Jack Canfield

One who understands and practices the law of attraction will get plenty.

Have you ever noticed that some people are born with Midas touch? Everything they do turns into gold! While there are others who continuously lose. Failure is part of their life.

Why does this happen? It is because of a simple reason that successful people create their success. Such people are well-informed about the 'law of attraction'.

They know what they want and how to get it from the universe. They attract success by focusing on the process and believing in the universe.

"Love the process, not the product.
Believe in the universe.
And you are bound to succeed."

—Dr. Kunal Banka

The other day, I was coaching one of my mentees. He was very curious to know about the law of attraction.

He asked me, "Sir, if the law of attraction is so powerful, then why is it that everyone is not benefitted from it?"

I replied, "To implement the law of attraction, you have to understand it in totality and believe in the power of the universe.

At the same time, you cannot leave everything to the universe. You have to work towards it and get into the process.

Most of the people don't understand this and the law itself."

The law of attraction is the most simple and fundamental law which guides everything in this universe. Yet surprisingly, very few people know about it. In fact, the law of attraction is so scientific that the whole universe is automated by this law. Anything can be achieved with this law. The power of the human mind and universe combined is more mighty than any source of energy on this planet.

This law simply means that like attracts like. The same is true for our thoughts. Like thoughts attract like results. This is the power of our brain.

Let me simplify this even more for you. Imagine that our brain is a powerful transmitter. It transmits to the universe. In return, the universe conspires to give us what we relay.

This is the reason why some people keep getting poor and are always in need, and a few in our society keep reaping rewards, even if they don't work so hard. Those who succeed always understand the law of attraction and gratitude, while others don't.

History is full of great scientists and other highly successful people who understood the law of attraction and practiced gratitude. They combined this with their hard work, and the recipe for success was ready and hence they succeeded.

Friends! This is the secret formula to success. But do we practice it? Most of us don't. However, in this book, we will understand exactly how this law works and how can we implement it in our lives easily to accelerate towards success.

Everything we think comes back to us. The universe receives it and gives us what we want. If we always complain about something, the universe returns the reason to complain a bit more. For example, if we keep complaining about our health, then it becomes worse and worse.

If we keep thinking about the bad things that happened to us in our past, our brain transmits the signal to the universe to bring more bad like the past. And the universe complies and gives us more bad things.

The universe or the supreme intelligence around is very giving. It never holds back and gives in abundance. If we ask for bad even unintentionally, it will give us bad. But if we learn to ask for good things, the universe will multiply the good and give us exactly what we want.

We will get lots of money, or luck or success, or anything we wished for.

Let's understand it at the levels of quantum physics. The whole universe is made up of energy. Everything is energy. Some energy is visible and some can't be seen.

The visible part of energy includes our physical possessions and needs only 5% of brain usage. The rest 95% of our brain can be used to channel the invisible energy.

This invisible energy is the communication with the universe and its reply.

Good energy attracts good and positive energy, and vice versa. If we channelize this good energy, we can definitely get all the good energy including the physical energy forms like money, material possessions, success and many more good things which are present in abundance, but we can't reach them due to our negative mindset.

We just have to use our brain to channelize our thoughts and learn to communicate with the energy of the universe, and nothing will be impossible for us.

We don't have anything to lose by understanding and practicing the law of attraction. There is a whole new world, full of abundance and richness waiting for you!

Our every thought creates a vibration in the universe and that comes back to us. If you need money, you should think…. I am rich. I am the richest person on this big blue marble. I have lots of money. Or you can think of any amount of money you want… I have x million rupees/dollar.

If you want good health, think that you are perfectly healthy. You are in the best of your health. Or if you want to improve any relationship, just think that… that person is so good and lovable…, etc.

When you are thinking these thoughts, feel them as if they are true. Imagine that you are having that thing or living your dream life in detail. By doing so, you are creating good vibrations which the universe, by law, will reflect to you in a way of manifestation of your wishes.

If you can think of it, you can have it physically. That's the whole truth of the 5% successful people in this world.

If you understand and practice the law of attraction, you can change your life, the way I have changed mine in the last 1 year.

My life had come to a standstill, and I was seeing a negative trend in my life.

I found myself in troubled waters as my finances were spiraling down, my health was out of control and I was gaining weight.

My mental health was really bad. I was always stressed and was left directionless. I wanted to run away. The fighter in me was long lost. In short, I was living a below-mediocre life.

Then one day, I happened to read a book called The Secret by Rhonda Byrne. In those days, Dr. Pallavi Kher was doing a book reading session on the same book. I attended that as well.

Those sessions and the wisdom in the book changed my way of perceiving myself and everything around me. The whole mindset changed, and I formed new habits, like my morning rituals.

Gradually, I could see things moving upwards.

Money, work and health all improved. I started making the maximum of my day and the wisdom available. I started believing that the world has a beautiful abundance, and it is all there for me to take!

I never looked back after that. The law of attraction gave me everything I needed and wanted. Yes, it was a reward for many, many micro-actions I took subsequently.

EXERCISE

1. Make a list of all things you want to get in life.

2. Make a list of all the things you do and say throughout the day, which send a negative message to the universe.

3. Consciously avoid doing the things mentioned in step 2.

4. Try to think and speak in positive terms throughout the day.

4. Thinking and speaking positively should become a lifelong habit.

CHAPTER SEVEN

BRAHMA MUHURAT- THE TIME FOR TREASURE HUNT

*"The potential of creation is at its peak between
0400 hours to 0530 hours before sunrise.*

*You can create all that you want very easily -
new knowledge, new skills, built health, develop yourself,
find solutions - you will get it at this time."*
—Sachin Ramdas Bharatiya

It was Sam's birthday. By the way, Sam is a friend of a close friend. My friends wanted to celebrate and I was also invited to the party. The celebration started early, at 7 pm. Everyone was enjoying it.

The moment I peeped into my watch, I noticed it was 8:45 pm. So, I decided to leave the party.

My close friend Z saw me leaving.

"Hey man, why are you leaving so early? You don't have patients at night."

I answered calmly, "I am going on a treasure hunt! And I am assured of the reward. In fact, I have accumulated lots of treasure so far."

Z gave me a disbelieving look. "Are you drunk?"

I replied with a smile, "You know I never drink. But if you want, I can show you how to get the treasure."

"YESSS… please take me too…" came the eager reply.

And both of us started walking towards our building. We lived in the same apartment.

I asked Z on our way, "Do you know what treasure I am talking about? Or what is the real treasure?

"Money man… money… That's the treasure… what else?"

"No Z. You are talking like the average people on this planet. To get the real treasure, you have to look beyond money and within yourself. It's hidden in your brain."

Now Z was getting angry. "What? Kunal, you wasted my time…, I was enjoying the party so much."

The next morning, Z came to my home at 8 am, his face dripping with curiosity.

"Please tell me the secret of you sleeping early and waking up early."

"Hmmm… now you are right on track. Come, sit and I will give you the secret."

I gave him a bunch of sheets that I had written for my book. It read as follows:

The first step toward a life-changing experience is the toughest one! Yes, it's to wake up early. Now I am not asking you to suddenly start waking up early from 8 am to 5 am. That will be too tough on you. I rather suggest that you make it early only by 30 minutes in the first week. This way, it won't be too challenging for you. But remember, all good things are tough to imbibe, but the end product is sweeter than God's nectar!

Next week, wake up half an hour earlier. Try to wake up at 5 am by the end of 30 days. For this, you will have to bring radical changes to your lifestyle, which you might think are impossible. But remember that you have to follow my suggestion only for a month and then you will find a new you, and you will start loving it. You will fall in love with your new routine as well as with yourself. Remember, the most important thing of all is that you have to love yourself indefinitely. The moment you start loving yourself, you become one with the universe, and then there will be no one to stop you. And it's too small a price to pay for a wonderful present and future.

Now, why am I asking you to wake up early? I know you will have to sacrifice your late-night parties, binges, socials, etc., but in the end, it's all worth it. Staying awake until late at night is the seed of diseases in the human body and also your productivity goes down if you try to work late at the night.

Waking up early is the most important step in transforming yourself. Why? Firstly, it gives you the extra time, the extra hour, which you always craved for. You do your most productive tasks early in the morning. It sets the tone of your day and energizes your existence. It has been proven that early risers are more productive throughout the day and they are filled with more energy.

The above-mentioned reasons are common ones, and everyone knows them. Now here is the real deal about waking up early... have you heard about Brahma Muhurat? I am sure you must have. According to Hindu mythology, Lord Brahma is the creator and this time of the day is named after him. So, this early hour is the time of creation. It is the time when worldly disturbances are not there. Our mind is fresh and not layered by the burden of the day ahead. It is at this time when we can connect with the universe perfectly, we can communicate with the universe and create whatever we want. We can understand this with the example of two points far apart on a road. One is our home or origin and the other is our destination. Now, at the peak traffic hour, if we drive on this road, it will take a lot of time to reach there, but if the road is empty, then we can travel the distance very fast.

In the same way, without disturbances, we can raise our frequency to the levels of the universe and vice versa. The universe also communicates with us faster at this time... thus, we, with the help of the universe, can create anything we want. We can get what we think of at this time. We only have to believe in ourselves, the universe, and we have to creatively visualize.

Have you ever wondered why, in all religions, morning prayers are very important? The simple reason is that it's in the morning when we can connect to the universe very easily and our frequency can match with that of the universe.

In fact, the majority of high performers are early risers.

Z read the whole manuscript in one go, and I could see his eyes widening with realization.

"Kunal, you should start doing TED Talks. I am sure you can change many lives."

I smiled and said, "My friend, I am already giving TED Talks and I have started the movement of a healthy body and a fit mind. I think you should join me in this movement."

"Yes, I am in, and I am so excited to start a super life. How do I start?"

I jawed, "Just do as I say for the next 30 days and witness the revolution in your life."

I gave him an exercise, which is recommended for you as well.

EXERCISE

1. Start a diary and daily mark your time of waking up.

2. Just after waking up, practice meditation. After meditation, record your feelings in your diary.

3. Do this for 30 days.

CHAPTER EIGHT

MEDITATE - LISTEN TO YOUR MIND

"Meditation is not about stopping thoughts, but recognizing that we are more than our thoughts and our feelings."
—Arianna Huffington

"With meditation, you become a sensitized superhero, completely in control, with endless possibilities at your fingertips."
—Tara Stiles

I was an average man with a mediocre thought process and way of living. I was happy until…

… one day I realized what is it I truly want in my life.

How did I recognize myself? It's a small story from my life.

In the year 2020, covid had taken over our lives and I was rendered jobless with no patients and no money. There was a lot of space in my brain to do the thinking.

I was trying to figure out what's the point of working like a machine for 13 years if I can't sustain an emergency like covid?'

I mean, I was financially and mentally broken.

One day, I was sitting alone in my room depressed, watching through the window. It had just rained and the trees and grass all were looking so fresh.

And at that moment, I felt a sense of immense peace within me. I had never felt like that.

I had connected with myself for the first time in my life. That was my first meditation moment.

Maybe it was the natural setting or my mental state. Whatever it was, it was a sense of pure peace and joy.

I could see my thoughts passing by. And that day onward, I started a movement in my life.

THE MEDITATION MOVEMENT

I started to meditate every day. I tried different techniques and, most important of all, I was a different man.

My anger vanished from my daily life. Within 6 months, no problem looked big enough to trouble me.

I developed an ice-like attitude. Always cool and in joy.

This helped me reach my titanium mindset. I became more mindful. Have you ever found bliss in the smallest of things?

The simple joy of coming home to your loved ones after a hard day of work... we do it as routine, but it has joy. I request you to take a pause and feel it.

The sheer joy of breathing in a gulp of fresh air can't be expressed.

The mirth of a warm blanket on a cold night or the mirth of having a roof above your head or the comfort of having clean water to drink.

All the happiness is out there. We only have to open our eyes to make it our own.

This was a lesson for me that helped me to come out of my misery. And due to some strange laws of attraction and physics, when you start enjoying small-small things, good news comes to you. You get bigger opportunities to be joyful.

This is why I want you to incorporate meditation into your DNA. That magical life is just a step away, and meditation is the step that takes you closer to that magical life and yourself.

Upon waking up early in the morning, you will realize the calmness of the crack of dawn and this is the time when you can listen to yourself very clearly. So, I highly recommend that you start the journey of your wonderful day by meditating early in the morning. Meditation is the best way to know and identify yourself.

Imagine a very calm mind, where you can see your thoughts and analyze them. I cannot express that tranquility in words. For me, it is this state of mind where I find solutions to my problems. This is so peaceful! Meditation is just as addictive as any drug minus the side effects. Actually, it is the much-needed mental exercise that we often miss.

You may say that meditation is boring and not your type of thing. Justifiable.

But you like a dish only when you taste it. Therefore, have the taste of meditation and then you will realize how much you have missed.

It's not simple, but it's not tough as well. The best part is you don't have to feel any particular way in meditation. Feel what you feel and as you feel. You will be amused by your thoughts and the monkey mind, which you never knew existed. After a few days of practice, you will be able to see your thoughts passing by like clouds and you will have control over whether to indulge in your thoughts or to let them go.

There is one simple technique for beginners in meditation. Just focus on breathing. Feel your breath coming in, feel the cold air rushing in, feel the air in your lungs reversing and coming out warm.

Just focus on your breathing sensation and let the thoughts come and go. Just observe your thoughts and let them go. Don't indulge in the stories your brain throws at you.

Just hold on to your breath and practice this every day without fail for one month. Once you start getting good at this, then you can proceed to the advanced stage of meditation.

You can get several apps, tutorials on YouTube, etc. to learn advanced meditation.

During your meditation practice, you don't have to feel in any particular way. Just be what you are and that's the beauty of meditation... you discover your true self and then you can improve upon yourself.

There are numerous advantages of meditation. It is an exercise for the brain. It cools your temper and makes you more resilient and patient. It heals your soul! Meditation is food for the brain and soul. It has done wonders for scores of successful people in the world. For me, meditation always opens new doors. it should become a way of life. Meditation is better than any anti-depressant!

"A most useful approach to meditation practice is to consider it the most important activity of each day. Schedule it as you would an extremely important appointment, and unfailingly keep your appointment with the infinite."
—Roy Eugene Davis

EXERCISE

1. Fix a time every day for 10 minutes to meditate. It should be a time and place where no one disturbs you for 10 minutes.

2. Every day, for the next 30 days, enter your meditation log in your accountability diary.

CREATIVE VISUALIZATION

*"Visualize the most amazing life imaginable to you.
Close your eyes and see it clearly. Then hold the vision for as
long as you can. Now place the vision in God's hands
and consider it done."*
—Marianne Williamson

Daydreaming is what they call it! For ages, our elders kept telling us… stop daydreaming. Daydreaming won't take you anywhere.

What if I tell you that dreaming is good? Daydreaming is still better!

Surprised?

All the inventions that have happened in the history of mankind were first dreamt in the minds of our great scientists. And then they became real.

First, you have to think and imagine what you want, and then it becomes real.

Or we can say that "whatever we think can be held in our hands".

So dream every day, but in a systematic manner. Here I am going to tell you a technique that will help you dream and make your dreams come true. This is called creative visualization.

As a dental surgeon, I face lots of challenges. There are a few operations that are really tough and get me worried. One such patient came into my clinic.

He was very apprehensive about dental treatment and was scared of our treatments. He needed a wisdom tooth to be extracted. I explained to him the process, and he agreed to the treatment. We scheduled his surgery for the next morning.

But in the back of my mind, I knew that the patient was very scared, and the procedure was going to be tough. I was really worried about him.

On the morning of the surgery, I sat back in silence after my meditation practice. I imagined with closed eyes that I was performing the surgery and I could see it happening in front of my eyes.

I visualized that the surgery went very well, and the patient was very happy. I could feel the emotions after doing a great surgery. I silently thanked the universe and opened my eyes.

That day, the surgery really went very well, and the patient got some more work done on his teeth as well. It was a real pleasure.

This is the power of visualization.

This is not a one-off incident. I do visualizations on a daily basis for a lot more things. And most of the time, they are accurate.

Now you may ask, how is this possible?

My friends, this is the power of visualization. It's based on pure science. Quantum physics explains all this.

Let me try to elaborate on this. Although quantum physics is a complicated matter, I have tried to simplify it and present it in my own way.

Quantum physics says everything is energy. What we think is also energy. When we think very clearly and see things happening in the eyes of the mind, our brain emits energy.

That energy reaches the energy of our universe and if it matches the frequency of universal energy, it comes back to us at a greater speed and intensity.

This energy influences the energy around us and, in turn, creates events that make our visualizations true.

So we need to have very strong visualization intensity to get things done.

Here is a step-by-step technique that I practice for my visualizations.

1. Sit back in a quiet place, preferably in the early morning. I have already explained the importance of Brahma Muhurat in Chapter 7.

   Do your meditation at least for 5-10 minutes.

2. Now chose one thing you want to get done, or chose one goal.

    Close your eyes and focus on that one goal. Imagine that your desired outcome is happening in front of your eyes.

    See it like a movie happening in front of you.

3. Now step in the movie. Be a part of that movie. See what you are doing and feel it. You should be doing things that you want to do. See the colors around you, feel the smell and everything you would when you would receive it in your real life.

    Remember that it's very important to feel, see and emote in the right way as it multiplies the energy you are emitting towards the universe.

4. By now, you must be emotionally charged and feeling happy about achieving your goals.

    Many times, I get tears of joy after this practice.

5. Now say thank you to this universe with all your heart for getting your wish true.

6. Slowly open your eyes and consider your work done. Feel that positive energy throughout your day.

Carry this energy the whole day and start working towards your goals. No one can stop you.

Now you must be thinking if it's so easy, why can't everyone use this technique to get whatever they want? There should be no scarcity in this world.

But that's not true. Knowing is different and practicing is different. And at the same time, the correct way to practice is the key.

But before practicing this method, we have to come out of a few stubborn thought patterns.

"I know this... it doesn't work"

"I tried it. It's not good"

"This is not the right thing to do"

Etcetera.

You have to open your mind to new things. Let me tell you that if you are reading this, then you have won half the battle.

Reading this book means you want changes in your life and you want a magical life. Now you just have to start believing. If you don't believe you can, you will not get the results… it holds true for all the fields in life.

Trust and belief go a long way to give results. The best example is the doctor-patient relationship. It's always true that whenever you trust your doctor, you get cured very fast. And the moment trust disappears, treatment becomes tough and results elusive.

Trust this knowledge, method and thought process behind the visualization.

Apart from quantum physics theories, creative visualization works on psychological levels as well. When we visualize ourselves in a position we dream of, our brain is charged up, and hormones cause such a wonderful effect on our body that positivity surrounds us and we are able to achieve much more.

Such is the power of controlled daydreaming.

Once we start believing, the next step is involvement.

The process of visualization should be done every day for a very long time. I would say it is a life-long process, but with different goals at different times.

During the visualization process, you should be totally involved in the thought and sight. You should feel and see every emotion and color as if it were for real. If you don't reach this stage, then your visualization is going wrong and you are wasting time.

The role of meditation cannot be undermined. If we meditate before visualization, our mind is already calm and it will be very easy for us to focus on the goal which we are visualizing.

Our goal can be anything. It may be the most outrageous thing you can think of. But you have to trust yourself and your goals.

If you support yourself, you don't need anyone else to support you.

If you can feel the emotions and engage your five senses in your visualization, then you have won the battle.

The next step comes after this. It is the most important one. Just after a good visualization, you have to believe that the universe has registered your request, and it's on your way and will reach you in due time.

And then your day starts. It's time to complement your visualization with some great mega action. If you don't take any action, any amount of thinking and daydreaming won't be useful.

No dream can be fulfilled without massive action.

MULTIVERSE

This is a fascinating theory put forward by modern physicists.

According to this, multiple realities and the universe exist at the same time. For e.g. Let's take the example of a businessman flying to London for a great business deal. There are multiple possibilities for this mission.

He may fly and clinch the deal successfully/he may fly but the deal may not be successful/he may miss the flight/his flight may crash and so on and on and on.

According to multiverse theory, all these possibilities exist at the same time in parallel universes.

But what we live is guided by our actions, visualizations, thought process and focus.

When we visualize, we direct all our mental energies towards our favorite possibility. So visualization is a very scientific method based on science which we still trying to understand.

The science is tough, but the process is simple and very effective.

It's a very strong tool to get you to that magical life which is enjoyed by a rare breed of people on this planet.

> *"I believe in creative visualization."*
> **—Victoria Beckham**

EXERCISE

Chose a goal for your life and visualize it daily, at least for the next 30 days and more, if needed. Follow the process explained above and try to get results.

CHAPTER TEN

READING- FOOD FOR THE BRAIN

"A reader lives a thousand lives before he dies, said Jojen.
The man who never reads lives only one."
—George R.R. Martin, A Dance with Dragons

When I was around 5-6 years old when I got my first taste of reading books. At that time, my father got me lots of story books and comics.

My favorite gift on my birthdays was books. For me, it was a different world where I spent my childhood. My father sowed the seeds of a huge tree which has blossomed and helped me in my worst times.

The next inspiration was my principal of the boarding school in Shimla. She told us to read at least one book a month other than textbooks. By this time, reading was in my DNA. I took her advice too seriously.

We were given Rs. 70 every month, and we could do anything we wanted with that money. Many of my friends watched movies, bought ice creams and enjoyed. For me, I had to buy a novel for Rs. 20 every month. I spent the rest of the money on lunch and come back to the hostel.

Reading those novels gave me a very broad outlook. My thinking, language and perception changed forever.

For this, I will always be grateful to my father and our principal, Dr. Sarita Singh.

Reading continued even in my busy years of medical school and beyond. But the real deal came when I was out of work and wretched. It was the year 2020; the covid year.

I read a great book called The Magic by Rhonda Byrne.

Then came The Secret by the same author.

These two books changed my life forever. And then a flurry of good books started coming into my universe, developing me as a human being.

Post that came the burning desire to share my learnings with the whole world and help others.

The result is this book in your hands. Such is the impact of reading!

There was a juncture in my life, as I have also mentioned in the previous chapters, when I was totally clueless about the direction of my life and was surrounded by lots of problems.

I overcame them all. But how?

It was not an overnight magic. It was a steady nourishing of my mind, which gave me the power and knowledge to face life and make it magical.

This grooming comes from reading books and reading lots of books. During the time of crisis, I turned to a lot of books and, like true friends, they helped me through the turmoil.

At the end of this book, I have suggested a list of books. They are the books that I read in my swamp days.

If it was not for these books, much of the magic of my life would have been missing. Books are the food for the brain. The better you feed your brain, the more polished it will be.

If we feed our brain with negative literature, we will get negative returns.

What does a book do? Firstly, it expands our horizon of thinking.

We get a new perspective and new thoughts. The moment we learn things beyond our scope of vision, we start becoming legends. The more we read, the more we create.

Human history has many such examples of great writers who were great readers.

"I believe that reading and writing are the most
nourishing forms of meditation anyone has so far found.
By reading the writings of the most interesting minds in
history, we meditate with our own minds and theirs as well.
This, to me, is a miracle."
—Kurt Vonnegut

This creation is not just limited to writing, but it also means the transformation of one's life.

Reading is as necessary for the mind as eating for the body. Our brain is highly underutilized.

Reading magnifies the efficiency of the brain and allows our mind to soar high in the world of imagination, which ultimately is visualization in serious terms.

Reading gives us the necessary knowledge to succeed in life. After all, we cannot assume that we know everything. A person's mind starts dying the day he assumes that he knows everything.

This mindset will lead to a painful decline in the mental health, physical health and the health of the soul.

To succeed in life, we need our brain to be at a frequency that is at the level of our universe. Only then can we transform our dreams into a reality.

And this frequency feeds on what we read, listen and think. If we eat very oily and fried food, our body tends to be sick. We develop several health problems. But if we eat healthily, we see that age becomes just a number. We stay very healthy and young!

Likewise, our mind's health depends on what we read and our intake of media. So it's very important to read good books which help us grow and expand our horizons of thinking.

If we read healthy literature, our brain tends to be very productive for growth. I read two books at any given time! One book is always a self-development, motivational or very positive book and the other is fiction which refreshes my mind.

I try to finish two titles every month. The morning times are for the motivational/self-help books and after dinner, I read fiction of my choice for 30 mins. So for me, it's 30 minutes in the morning and 30 minutes in the evening. This routine keeps my mind positive and refreshed.

And you can do it too! Initially, you don't have to read for 30 minutes… just start with 10 pages of a book each day. But I want a commitment from you that you will do it for at least 30 days in a row.

Be honest to yourself, believe in this routine and just do it. You don't know your hidden side, which will surprise you and the people around you.

Commit to yourself that you will read every morning after your meditation. This will stimulate your brain to a new level. You will see various new ideas flowing out that you never knew existed.

This is very compelling because if you feed your brain well and give it a splendid exercise, there is no power in the world that can stop you from succeeding.

Raise the frequency of your mind to such levels that you resonate with the universe. Be in such a mental state that no one can defeat you. And it's very rightly said:

"All battles are first won or lost in mind."

—Joan of Arc

So let's prepare ourselves for that BULLET PROOF mindset where there is no limit to success.

Reading will give you knowledge, strategy and the road to success.

"If one cannot enjoy reading a book over and over again, there is no use in reading it at all."

—Oscar Wilde

"I find television very educating. Every time somebody turns on the set, I go into the other room and read a book."
—Groucho Marx

EXERCISE

1. Make a list of books of your choice or take the help of the suggested reading section and make your list.

2. Mark your timings in the day when you want to read.

3. Make it a point to read at least 20 pages a day.

4. Make a note of your reading in your accountability diary.

CHAPTER ELEVEN

EXERCISE TO A CHAMPION BODY

"Strength does not come from physical capacity. It comes from an indomitable will."
—Mahatma Gandhi

"If you don't make time for exercise, you'll probably have to make time for illness."
—Robin Sharma

Recently, I went on a trek with an old friend. He was too excited to do a trek as he said that he wanted some exercise. As far as I know, he had never exercised.

He had a huge belly, and he loved to drink!

We started our trek in the morning at around 6 am. We were supposed to walk through a jungle and it was a 3-hour hike.

Ten minutes after we started, we found ourselves climbing on a slightly steep trail. Suddenly, my friend asked me to stop. I looked at him, he was panting like a crazy person and dropped to his knees.

"I can't go any further. Please let's go back."

I had anticipated this behavior, as I knew his fitness levels were very bad.

I stopped, and we decided to get back home.

Once we reached home, I asked him to stay back for breakfast and he readily agreed.

I said in a serious tone, "Do you know what happened today?"

He was totally ignorant of his state. He simply replied, "My age caught up with me."

I was not surprised by his reply, as there are many in our society, in fact, 90% of us, who are like my friend… making an excuse when it comes to fitness.

I said, "My friend, even I am of the same age as yours, I run for 5 km a day and I am fitter than you! Where is the difference?

The difference is in our attitude towards our health and fitness. I treat my body as a temple and I nourish it accordingly. And I strongly recommend the same to you.

It's a shame that most of us never exercise and don't have any control over our eating habits. The modern human being should be very much aware of his health and how to nourish his body."

My friend uttered in despair, "Bro, it's not that I have not tried to be fit. But it never works for me. I don't know how to do it. Can you help me?"

I told him about my mentorship program and he readily agreed to join it.

I gave him some script to read before starting.

The text of that script read as follows:

"Now comes the time for nourishing our body. Because we already know that health is wealth.

But how many people use this knowledge in their favor?

These days, we see rampant diseases caused by unhealthy lifestyle like BP, diabetes, heart diseases, obesity, psychological disorders, dental disorders, fatty liver, etc. We are seeing more and more young people falling into heart attacks. Why is this happening, if we know that health is wealth?

The reason is ignorance of people and reluctance to improve.

And the mindset which doesn't allow one to be consistent in exercise. Most people join the gym and drop out in a month.

So we need uncontaminated willpower to improve our health. If we enrich our health, then the battle is already half won!

Now what I want you to do is, after you accomplish your morning task of reading, commit one hour to your body for the next 30 days.

Exercise has manifold benefits. It keeps your body fit, removes excess fat, improves the health of your heart and releases hormones in your body that make you feel good and relieved of all stress.

When I talk about exercise, I don't mean a slow walk in the park without a single bead of sweat on your forehead.

When you exercise, you should perspire, and your heart rate should be elevated. However, first, consult your doctor before taking up any rigorous exercise.

Your exercise hour can be anything from a run, jog, walk to the gym or yoga or Zumba or anything which causes you to sweat.

Once you taste the fun of exercise, you will be addicted to it... the good addiction! Do it every morning.

Try to mix and match various forms of exercise on different days, as the mind gets bored and the body gets used to the same exercise every day.

You will see a radical shift in your health and energy levels in a month's time. During the exercise, if you see someone with a really good body, don't lose faith in the workout.

Just be grateful and say in your mind... thank you for such a perfect body I have. Always imagine yourself in your best form and the body form you want to attain. This will help you reach your goal faster. (inspired by The Magic by Rhonda Byrne)

Have faith and persistence. This and only this will take you towards your goal.

Have you ever seen a man suffering from a lot of lifestyle diseases? Just imagine yourself in his shoes for a second. Will you like to live like him forever? Or do you want to be fit enough to enjoy the abundance of life?

Only if we are fit can we enjoy the abundance of life uninhibited. Only a healthy body can have a healthy mind, and only a healthy mind can take care of a healthy body.

You can even indulge in a sport that involves physical activity. I love playing cricket and table tennis. In spite of my busy schedule, I find time for physical activities and so should you if you want to open doors to the new you! And trust me, the new you is going to be a much, much better version of your current self. You don't have anything to lose but a world of bounties to gain. THE GIFT OF HEALTH IS THE BIGGEST GIFT IN THIS WORLD.... ask those who are in bad health. They are willing to give anything in barter for good health.

And the best part is that you cannot stop aging, but you can slow down the process! How? By exercising and eating wholesome foods! It's so simple and yet we see hospitals full of patients with lifestyle diseases. Have you ever seen a movie star who never ages? There are many... and now you too know the secret!

Let me explain to you how exercise helps in slowing down aging. There is a structure attached to our DNA at the microscopic levels called TELOMERES. When telomeres reduce in size, one starts aging.

Exercise stops the reduction in the size of telomeres, thus prolonging the life span. At the same time, there are multiple hormones that are released during exercise which make us healthy and give our brain a power boost. This has been very beautifully explained in the book The 5 am Club by Robin Sharma. I suggest you to read it thoroughly and it can change the way you live and think. So go ahead and read this book!

DIET

Now comes a very important part of our lives… food! Let me ask you: Can a diesel car run on petrol? Or a petrol car on diesel? No… right? So, how can our body survive on foods and drinks that are not made to be consumed? Yes, I am talking about the foods we eat these days.

Our breakfast comes out of packets in the form of cereals. Our kids take all the junk food like noodles and pasta to school for tiffin and we, grownups, are never tired of fried food. Every cup of tea in our offices is accompanied by either samosas or pakoras. Our sweet tooth compels us to have tea and coffee as a religious ceremony in the office… sometimes, I wonder how our health is going to be in 10 years' time.

Already, obesity is spreading like a pandemic in our younger population. And then after stuffing those yummy pizzas and burgers, we complain of extra kilos, expanding waistline, diabetes, BP and all sort of diseases.

If we want a better and fitter version of ourselves, we have to immediately change our food habits.

Have you heard 'WE ARE WHAT WE EAT'?

Where do we start… Let's begin with our breakfast. Our food should contain proteins, vitamins and carbohydrates in a balanced amount and our Indian diet is very balanced in that aspect. Eat local produce and freshly cooked edibles. Avoid packaged food as much as possible.

Eat rotis or any traditional Indian breakfast which is full of nutrients. Be it dalia, idli, dosa, parathas, or poha. Don't eat so much fat that your arteries cannot clean it. Eat good fat like dry fruits, roasted seeds, eggs, ghee and so on.

Yes, ghee should be an integral part of life as it has multiple benefits. One tablespoon of ghee in every meal won't do any harm but will give a lot of good fats. It is conducive for skin, eyes, joints, brain and whatnot. Ghee is a doctor on our plate if taken in moderation. That's our granny's wisdom!

Mid-meal snacking is another problem we face, as these mid-meals are laced with oil or sugar. Instead, we can opt for nuts, dry fruits, bananas or any raw fruit as our mid-meal replacement.

Lunch should again be balanced and should include some rice or rotis, dal and salads with some veggies. Here the mention of rice brings to my mind the strict instructions of many diet schools that rice is the villain! Trust me, it's not. It won't make you fat if taken in the right portions and with the right vegetables and fruits.

Coming to the most important meal of the day… dinner.

Most of us use this dinner time to watch TV and eat… we often watch the news… mostly negative or watch the daily sops. Food becomes secondary and TV becomes primary!

Do you remember the last time when you ate your food with mindfulness, without any distractions and enjoyed the taste of every bite? I am sure it was a long time ago. I suggest making your dinner time the family time where the whole family sits and eats together, present with each other, not only physically but mentally as well. Switch the TV off. The negativity and distractions of TV keep lingering in our mind even after we sleep. This draws our subconscious mind to negativity and emits negative energy, thus, attracting the negatives to us.

There is an ancient ritual in India and many other cultures of praying before eating. However, we have very conveniently done away with the ritual in the modern era. But that prayer is very important as we offer our gratitude to the universe for getting the food on our plate. In this prayer, we appreciate that this food is going to nourish our body. This is a scientific fact that our thoughts alter the nurturing value of our food.

Study: Dr. Masaru Emoto, the Japanese scientist who revolutionized the idea that our thoughts and intentions impact the physical realm, is one of the most important water researchers the world has known. For over 20 years until he passed away in 2014, he studied the scientific evidence of how the molecular structure in water transforms when it is exposed to human words, thoughts, sounds and intentions.

The extraordinary life work of Dr. Emoto has been documented in the New York Times Bestseller, The Hidden Messages in Water. In his book, Dr. Emoto demonstrates how water exposed to loving, benevolent, and compassionate human intention results in aesthetically pleasing physical molecular formations in the water. Whereas, exposure to fearful and discordant human intentions results in disconnected, disfigured, and "unpleasant" physical molecular formations. He did this through Magnetic Resonance Analysis technology and high-speed photographs.

Thus, I start every meal with a prayer of gratitude, and I eat with my family. I chew every bite slowly and mindfully. This helps highlight the real taste of food. You will be surprised how tasty your food is! Just follow this method and see the magic.

Wonder tip: Have you ever thanked your wife or mother for the food they cook for you unconditionally. Try it today at dinner, just thank them… and see the magic! Yes, it works.

Try to finish your food latest by 8 pm and keep a minimum gap of one and a half hours from the time of sleeping."

The next morning, my friend came home, and he was totally charged up.

"What an amazing text! How do you have so much knowledge?"

I answered, "It's my passion, as this has been taught to me by my mentor Dev Gadhvi."

For the next thirty days, I watched his transformation under my guidance, and it gave me immense happiness and satisfaction that I could help someone achieve a magical life.

EXERCISE

1. Wake up early.

2. Exercise daily for 60 minutes.

3. Journal what you are eating and at what time. This way, after a week, you will have a perfect idea of the improvement needed in your diet.

4. Follow the diet tips mentioned in the chapter.

5. Repeat all the steps for 30 days and see the change. Journal the change as well.

CHAPTER TWELVE

POST DINNER RITUALS

"Rituals enhance your ability to sweeten your life through something as simple as how you prepare for sleep."
—from **Sleep Rituals**:
100 Practices for a Deep and Peaceful Sleep

A majority of people who want to attain fitness, good mental and physical health fail in their efforts. Do you know why is that?

It is because they try at the wrong place. They refine their mornings and try to fit in their workouts. By the time their day comes to an end, they are so exhausted that the motivation for the next day seems impossible.

In my opinion, success in our morning routine starts in our evenings.

What we do, what we eat and what we consume as content decide what we do the next day.

For example, if we sleep early, only then we can wake early the next morning.

We ought to clear our mind of negativity.

Again, I would suggest staying away from screens. Screens emit blue light which inhibits melatonin, a hormone that induces sleep. No melatonin – no sleep. So stay away from screens and let your mind and body relax.

Switch your phones off before dinner. They are a big source of distraction and can cause social media toxicity and anxiety. This toxicity is the biggest problem of this age. In fact, we should detox every day from social media.

No TV after dinner. Again, it's the screen that emits blue light and the content which starts controlling your mind! We are supposed to control it and not be controlled by it. The negative content reinforces negative thoughts and subconsciously makes us negative. Dedicate this time for some exercise… maybe a brisk walk. Keep some time aside for family and kids and read at least 10 pages.

Too much to ask for? Well, you don't have anything to lose but a world to gain. Try it if you want to do what humans are made to do. Even animals sit, eat and sleep. But as human beings, it's your duty to make every day; every evening and every night beautiful.

I was a sedentary fool some time ago. I would come home from the clinic at 7 pm, eat, eat and eat and then do the family ritual of watching endless TV after dinner. After that, I would be worried if I would get a sound sleep or not. Every morning, I would look at my waistline and wonder if I would ever lose it. Nothing worked in my life. I was working and eating like a zombie, and was wasting my life. All the sharpness of my life and productivity became a remote thought.

I made those mistakes and paid for them. But you don't do it. I am sharing with you my years of experience. In a nutshell, I am giving you a shortcut to a healthy life and a better functioning brain. Don't keep yourself away from all the success, glory and beauty of life while hiding behind the screens! Come out and embrace life. You will wonder at the marvels of life and the beauty of the people around you.

So follow these steps:

1. Switch your phone off at dinner time.
2. No TV after dinner.
3. No social media…, it distracts and confuses the mind.
4. Spend some time with your family members.
5. Play with your children.
6. Engage in some physical activity like walking after dinner.
7. Meditate for 5 minutes before diving into your bed.

BEDTIME

This is the most important time of your day. This time decides your next day. How? Because whatever we do during and before bedtime influences our next day.

At bedtime, I would suggest that you recap all the events of the day and, in your mind, replay all the positive events. If something has gone wrong during the day, just replay it in the way you would have wanted it to happen. And then count your blessings for all the good things that happened to you that day. Say a big thank you for all the goodness in your life.

You can even write down a to-do list for the next day if you want.

When you do all this, what happens is that your brain subconsciously keeps your vibrations high.

The energy you have is so high that it starts to match that of the universe. This is when the miracle happens. The universe starts working for you even if you are sleeping and brings good to you.

Imagine if your brain is in the negative zone subconsciously while you are asleep, what will you attract? Negative things. This justifies the evening ritual.

Evening rituals are magical if practiced diligently and in a fun-filled manner. Spending quality time with family is the pinnacle of life. Being productive just by staying away from the screen is just a free promotion.

You may have excuses that you cannot stay away from your phone due to work or something else… But excuses are always excuses. Have the mindset of a winner and focus of steel, and you will be unstoppable in all aspects of life.

EXERCISE

This whole chapter is an exercise for you to follow for the next 30 days.

Maintain an accountability diary where, every day, you mention your evening ritual.

CHAPTER THIRTEEN

THE 8*3 FORMULA

"The gift of balance in your life—may you find the balance of life, time for work but also time for play. Too much of one thing ends up creating stress that no one needs in their life."
—Catherine Pulsifer

It was 7:30 pm, and blood was dripping from my gloved hands. I had just performed a very delicate dental surgery, and was relieved to see my patient getting cured.

Suddenly, my phone rang. It was my wife.

"When are you coming home?"

I said that it would take another hour, as I had three more patients to attend to.

That evening, I reached home at 11:30. The repercussions were obvious.

My wife was very upset about it.

I am sure you too must have treaded through a similar situation at some or other time in your life. Be it a doctor, executive, CEO or business owner, most of us face this. And then, what follows is a series of unhealthy relations, bad lifestyle, bad health and much more.

Do you think after doing all this hard work, we deserve to suffer the consequences I have mentioned above? NO is the only answer.

Then why does this situation arise?

We, as professionals or employees, work to get a good life. But we get a life full of question marks and misery. If we love our family and close ones so much, then we should spend more time with them instead of getting glued to work.

I realized this the tough way. I was a very busy practitioner and was engrossed in work, thinking it was my glory. I had developed cholesterol and was on the verge of acquiring many lifestyle diseases.

The detection of cholesterol was a wake-up call and the ultimatum from my wife was the final nail. I decided to change everything. I was born on this planet to enjoy riches and abundance; not to suffer at the hands of work and destiny.

I still remember that day when I decided to strike a balance in my life. That day changed me forever.

I want you too to learn from my mistakes and benefit from my self-discovery.

I decided to apply the 8*3 formula to my life and it magically sorted everything out. This formula simply states:

8 hours of work

8 hours of play

8 hours of sleep

Hence, 8*3. Is it difficult to understand? No. Still, many fail to fathom and accept it.

Everything in this world hangs on to a balance. The same is true for our lives. Our lives are a balance of work, play and sleep.

8 HOURS OF WORK

Easier said than done!

Yes. It's tough for us workaholics. How can we get everything wrapped up in 8 hours when 11 hours are also not enough to finish that work? How can we climb up that ladder of success by working for just 8 hours?

What if I tell you that we can achieve double work than our current status by working for lesser hours? Surprised? I have done it. I work for 6 hours a day and 6 days a week, and that too doesn't feel like work. Still, I have increased my income many folds.

And you can do it too. I followed simple steps, and I want you as well to follow this proven formula:

1. ***Prioritize***: Make a list of the work you want to do throughout your day. And then mark the most important 3 tasks. Finish them in the first 2 hours of your day. And then take on lesser important works.

I always keep my most important appointments from 10 am to 12 pm and attend to those patients with perfection.

2. *Delegate*: Make a list of all the work you can delegate. And you will be surprised to know that you can always delegate work, even if you find it impossible at this moment.

   When I am examining my most important patients, at the same time, my consultant doctors are doing other work in different OTs. That way, I get more work done at the same time without affecting productivity.

3. *Let go*: There are a lot of things you think you can't live without doing, but in reality, you don't need to waste time on useless things.

4. *Time audit*: I have discussed this in detail in the next chapter Manage Your Time like a Champion. Time audit is the most important tool to manage your time and get more out of it. You will again be surprised at how much time you are wasting on useless jobs.

8 HOURS OF PLAY

WORK HARD, PARTY HARDER. This has been my motto for so many years. We all need to rejuvenate and celebrate our success, even if it's a small victory.

Those who say that they have no time for family or themselves, I am offering you 8 hours for that!

We can utilize these 8 hours in two blocks, 5 pm to 9 pm and 5 am to 9 am.

These 8 hours should not be wasted on social media, binge watching and phone. I suggest you to keep a distance from your phone, social media and any kind of screen during these hours.

I call these 'recharge hours'.

These are the golden hours that form a solid base for the magical life we all dream of.

Use this time for exercising, reading, and spending some real quality time with your spouse, children and parents. They deserve this time of yours. Why?

SPOUSE

He/she sacrifices so much for you. Therefore, he/she needs that quality time with you. It can do wonders for your relationships.

CHILDREN

Our children are dearest to us. Their happiness fills us with immense joy. Their well-being and cheeriness are priceless.

We deserve their time. Before they grow into adults, why don't we spend every possible moment with them?

Never ever miss the opportunity of spending quality time with kids. You will be surprised at how your life becomes full of joy when you spend time with your kids.

PARENTS:

Most of us ignore our parents as they grow old. But remember, they are the tree that always gives us cool shade. Spending time with them is mandatory as our parents always bring selfless, nourishing energy into our lives.

We should make it a point to spend some time very frequently with our parents.

Their blessings are very important in our lives.

8 HOURS OF SLEEP

Sleeping for 8 hours a day is very necessary for a fit body and mind. Our body recharges and repairs itself while we sleep. Lack of sleep makes us lethargic and faulty at decision making. It also drives us toward heart diseases. Even oversleeping is not good for health as it causes many detrimental effects on health.

Follow this 8*3 rule and you will always flourish. Try to fit your life into this rule, not vice versa and you will see happiness pouring in from everywhere in this universe.

"Strive not to be a success, but rather to be of value."

—Albert Einstein

CHAPTER FOURTEEN

MANAGE YOUR TIME LIKE A CHAMPION

"He who every morning plans the transactions of that day and follows that plan carries a thread that will guide him through the labyrinth of the most busy life."
—Victor Hugo

Rahul, my neighbor, met me in the elevator. Lines of worry were evident on his face. I asked him what had happened.

"I don't have time for anything. My wife is always angry with me that I never give her time. Today I could not even go to my child's PTM.

I don't have time for the gym. My health is going downhill like anything. I can't do anything I want to. Life is so busy. I feel like running away."

I said to him, "running away is not the option. What will you run away from and where will you cut and run?"

Rahul scratched his head and said, "I don't know man… life feels like a dark tunnel with no sign of light at the end."

I suggested, "Don't worry Rahul, I will help you out. Meet me this Sunday at 9 am."

He just nodded unenthusiastically. But I knew he will come.

I am sure you can relate to Rahul and his life.

I have a deep connection with this situation.

On the following Sunday morning, Rahul was at my doorstep at sharp 9 am. He was in a bad shape physically and worse mentally. He looked like a caged animal waiting for a chance to escape…. from his life.

"Welcome to your freedom Rahul!" I said cheerfully. He was perplexed.

"What do you mean by freedom, doc?"

I returned, "So far, you have been the slave of your life and time. Now you will start working towards your freedom."

Rahul was still confused with a look on his face that explained his state of mind.

I made coffee with an omelet for both of us and we sat down on the terrace of my flat.

"You know Rahul… you remind me of my younger self. My previous version was exactly as you are today. I was working 10 to 8 Monday to Saturday in my clinic like a mad, possessed person. I had no time. I was so occupied with work that my wife once told me to put a bed in my clinic and that I should stay there only. No need to come home…"

Rahul stopped sipping his coffee midway.

"I can't believe that! Then how did you change your life? These days, you always have time and you work at your will."

"Rahul, it's important to own your time and life, and not vice versa. Today, most people are just being ruled by time and life. We should come out of this imprisonment and then we would realize that this world is full of wonders and abundance created just for us!

I followed a few simple things which changed me. You know it's too much fun to own your time. You can make this change in just 30 days if you follow my advice."

Rahul interjected and asked me wide-eyed, "Doc, is it really possible?"

I said, "Yes. Absolutely. First of all, you have to commit to me that whatever I am telling you, you will follow it for the next 30 days with blind faith."

OK was the response immediately.

I told him, "First of all, do a time audit for your day.

WHAT IS A TIME AUDIT?

A time audit is very simple. For the next 24 hours, just keep on noting everything that you do and make the entries honestly. I am asking you to do this because there are 24 hours in a day. If we sleep for 8 hours, we still have 16 hours, which is sufficient for everything we want to do. So go on and make the audit. Mark all the time wasters and you will be surprised to see that you have been leaking out a lot of time.

So go on and meet me tomorrow… with the audit diary."

Rahul slowly got up after finishing his coffee and walked out of my home in disbelief. He still had to rewire his belief system.

Three days later, Rahul showed up at my door at 8 pm. He was all surprised and his eyes were wide open. He animatedly entered my home and started in an excited tone…

"What a way you told me Kunal. You know, I have been wasting half my day on useless activities. I fritter away a lot of time on social media and binge-watching. I also party, eat out every night and sleep late. Thus, I wake up late and then rush through my day, and I am always under pressure."

"See, I told you, you can sort it out," I said.

"But how to eliminate these time wasters?"

I replied in a philosophical tone, "Whatever I am going to tell you in the next few minutes, just follow it unwaveringly for the next 30 days, and you will see the wonders of abundant time and health.

Firstly, stop using social media for the next 30 days. Just detox!"

I could see Rahul's face turning grey. "It's impossible for me to completely cut off from social media."

"Then make it possible Rahul… whatever it takes, just do it, and you will thank me forever."

"Ok" was all Rahul could mutter.

"Next," I said, "stop late-night partying so that you can sleep on time and also call a halt to binge-watching TV."

Rahul wanted to interrupt, but I waved him off and he smartly took the hint.

"Wake up early and do everything you wanted to… you can even go to the gym during that extra time!

Prioritize your day. See what's the most important thing you have to do on that day and do it first. Analyze what work needs not to be done or can be avoided.

Try to delegate work as much as possible in your workplace.

Focus on the most important task of the day and finish it.

Try to wrap up the most difficult and important task of the day before 12 pm."

"Ok… will give it a try for sure. Thanks, Kunal."

Rahul left my home with his heavy frame and a heavy heart. After all, I asked him to part with his favorite time killers.

Fast forward to 45 days.

It was a Sunday, and I was reading the book 6 Sundays a Week Life by my mentor, Dev Gadhvi. Suddenly, the doorbell rang. I opened the door and saw a beaming Rahul… he walked in and hugged me.

I was surprised by his enthusiasm and his leaner frame.

"What happened Rahul? You are looking too happy."

"Kunal… you are not just a good surgeon, but also a very good life doctor!

I followed all your advice and followed it to the word. It worked miracles for me and my family life. I am fitter physically and mentally as well.

I am the owner of my time. I am a free man and it's all because of your guidance."

This was the moment of the day. I felt so happy to help Rahul.

I wonder how many Rahuls are around but many don't get help.

I wish I could help and transform many, many more people!

"By failing to prepare, you are preparing to fail."
—Benjamin Franklin

EXERCISE

1. Do a time audit for your day.

2. Strike out all the time wasters.

3. Evaluate the free time available.

4. Delegate and focus.

5. Make a time journal and document your days for at least 30 days regularly, and keep dissecting your routine for a fitter and wiser you!

CHAPTER FIFTEEN

RELATIONSHIPS

"When we love, we always strive to become better than we are. When we strive to become better than we are, everything around us becomes better too."
—Paulo Coelho

I was flying in a spaceship. All alone. Through the window, I could see vast darkness decorated with tiny flecks of lights from distant stars. It all looked very beautiful. Suddenly, I realized that there is no one to talk to me and share the beauty of this scene with me. I was all alone in the vast expanse of the universe. I felt very lonely. My head started spinning and I felt dizzy. I screamed in intense agony!

Suddenly, I woke up with a start. I was drenched in sweat. But I was so relieved that I was on earth, in my bed, and my family members were around. This dream was a wake-up call. In the dark of night, I suddenly realized how important relationships are. Being alone sometimes is ok but being alone always is not right.

The next morning, I was on the phone, calling my old friends and I realized that we are so ignorant that we neglect our most important possession… our relations!

Be it our life partner, children, parents or friends, we need everyone to survive on this planet, in this society.

Health and wellness are all about health/wealth and relationships.

And this can be achieved by balancing and nurturing our mind, body and soul. Our relationships can be attached to our souls. The better relationships we have with our surroundings and people, the better souls we have.

And we all know that a better soul can do wonders. So relationships are very important in our life.

Have you ever thought about what a bad relationship can do to us? It's like a leech sucking our life from us. We are always filled with negativity towards that person. But we forget that all the negativity we have for others is, in fact, being directed at us by the universe, and that too with interest! So always be positive for others, even if they have wronged you. Just stay away from those people. Avoid all types of negativity.

Coming back to relationships, do you remember when you spent some quality time with your parents?

Parents are like the sun, always giving us warmth and energy. So we should always embrace their blessings and make it a point to spend some real quality time with them.

This is a priority as, without this ingredient, all your relations will be empty and futile. Relationship with parents have to be selfless and without expectations.

Just spend some time with your parents and see the joy in their eyes. Their happiness is priceless.

There was a time when I was too engrossed in work, working even on Sundays. And then I realized what was I missing on. I was at distant quarters from the real joy in life. The ladies of my life, my wife and daughter... I was missing their precious company.

Then one fine day, I decide that enough is enough. Now is the time to give more time to my loved ones and myself.

I also realized that the best relationships in the world are ones in which nothing is expected from both sides. A selfless relationship is one that makes really strong relations.

Just close your eyes and try to find those selfless relationships in your life... how many can you count?

For me, it was my parents, my wife and daughter and a couple of friends! I said to myself, "That's it?"

Sounds pathetic, right? But it's almost the same for most of us. So ideally, we should give more time and attention to these relationships.

But what can we do?

We take them for granted. We give less time to these particular relationships and we run behind the fake ones!

My friends... we have to change our priorities in life and look at our people without any filters. I have done this. You have to do it.

Recently, one of my uncles called me after a long time out of nowhere. All of a sudden, he started finding me adorable and claimed that he was my favorite uncle in childhood. And then came the intention… in the third call to me, he asked for money!

So, my dear fellows, any relationship where money is the basis and foundation is not worth pursuing. I blocked that uncle of mine and never talked to him again.

The same is true for friends. Recently, I went to Bangalore to meet my college friend who had flown in from the USA.

I went with my family and she was with hers. We spent two days with her, and during one conversation, my wife asked her, "Keerti, what made you and Kunal best friends?"

Keerti replied, "We never expected anything from each other and were always there for each other without any hidden motive."

This conversation gave a deep insight into the difference between real and fake friends and relations.

I hope, now you can understand what I am trying to convey. The whole point is to declutter your life from toxic people.

I agree that there are some close relations which sometimes are not in the best of health. For example, these days, we see adult kids having a lot of differences with their parents. Whenever we have differences with parents (differences are bound to happen between two living beings), sit down in a quiet place, take a paper and pen and just write ten points about your parents thanking them.

Just think, had they abandoned you after you were born, you would not be in the position to even have a respectable life!

When you finish ten points of gratitude towards your parents, just say a silent thank you, thank you and thank you.

This exercise will dissolve all the harsh feelings you have towards anyone. And they will also have good feelings towards you.

The same is with your spouse. Whenever you two have differences, just close your eyes, focus on your breathing and think about the time when that person did something good for you.

I am sure you will find many reasons to feel grateful for them. Just write those points in a diary. Read them over again and again.

Gradually, you would have negated all the negativity and the same would reflect from that person's behavior as well.

The rudest fact on this planet is that any relationship is worth its salt only when there are no expectations from each side. The moment expectations creep in, that relationship is spoiled.

> *"Indifference and neglect often do much more damage than outright dislike."*
>
> **—J. K. Rowling,**
> *Harry Potter and the Order of the Phoenix*

EXERCISE

1. Make a list of the 5 best relationships you have. Write 10 points of gratitude for each of them.

2. Make a list of 5 sour relations you have and again take your time to write 10 points of gratitude for each of them.

3. Read both the lists daily for the next 30 days and see the magic.

4. Write in a diary about how you want to be talked about when you are not present at the gathering.

CHAPTER SIXTEEN

MONEY MATTERS

"Before you speak, listen. Before you write, think. Before you spend, earn. Before you invest, investigate. Before you criticize, wait. Before you pray, forgive. Before you quit, try. Before you retire, save. Before you die, give."
—William A. Ward

It was March 2019. I still remember the panic in the air when the covid outbreak rocked. I never believed it to be so big. But against all my will and wishes, covid spread and a lockdown was imposed.

I had no idea of how the lockdown will be and how long it will last.

I was least prepared financially. I had no cash. I never had the habit of keeping cash, as the practice was on a roll.

Suddenly, patients stopped coming in. There was no revenue. I had only twenty thousand rupees in my hand. There was no money for staff salary.

On top of that, I had a loan of Rs. 1 crore in my name. The EMIs were causing a lot of heartburn. This phase of my life gave me a titanium mindset. I had no source of income and did not know how I would sail through this phase.

My situation was that of a fish without water. I thought, thought and thought. No respite. No ideas.

The creditors were calling every other day. I was scared every time my phone rang. So many times, I found myself staring at the roof, trying to find solutions to my problems.

There were days when I wanted to run away from everything. I was witnessing thoughts of suicide and helplessness. And to add insult to the injury, I could not share this with anyone, not with my wife, not with my parents. I did not want to burden them.

Amidst this hopelessness, one day, I was lying and gazing at the white ceiling fan. Suddenly one thought dropped anchor on my mind…. "Dude, you have a ceiling on your head in these testing times. You have a home to live in. At least be thankful for all you have and stop complaining."

This realization got me out of a deep state of dismay. That was the first time I felt gratitude for anything in my life. And then I thought, whatever may come, I have to prove to myself that I am worth it and I deserve a very good life.

This thought process made me believe in myself again. And this belief in ourselves is the tool that can do wonders. I started facing my problems head-on.

A few other things started happening in my life at the same time. I met some very learned teachers online, like Dr. Rajiv Verma and Dr. Sujit Pardeshi. They showed me the way of hope and how to fight it out. Three years later, I got a chance to meet Dr. Rajiv and thanked him for his support.

I also met Dr. Pallavi Kher online, who was conducting lessons on gratitude and secret. After attending her sessions, I started believing in myself and thinking in a different way. I imbibed the habit of practicing gratitude and visualizing my future. It worked wonders.

I was as if I could attract anything I wanted. I started taking calls from my creditors and assured them that I will pay it off very soon. And I kept my promise. I used my credit cards to settle all my outstanding payments.

Once the creditors were paid off, materials started coming into the clinic and I resumed my work. It was the middle of the covid phase, I had very few patients but I started campaigns for my covid free practice and gradually patients started coming in. Slowly, money also came in.

In the meantime, I also sold off a machine for which I had a loan of Rs. 60 lakhs. I was lucky to find a very supportive senior and mentor, Dr. Kuber Sood, who helped me sell it off. Although I sold it for a loss, but it lifted a heavy load off my shoulders.

For the next two years, every penny I earned, I used it to pay off my debts.

TWO AND A HALF YEARS LATER

I go to my clinic from 1 to 4, 5 days a week. I am never scared of losing money. Today, I live stress-free and I am loan-free. But what was my biggest takeaway? It was my money mindset.

My mindset toward money was wrong. I always watered the belief that I have made enough and that's my limit and that I should not be greedy. This is how we are programmed in our modern society from our childhood. Money is evil, we should not run after money, we should not ask! And it goes on. There are so many beliefs that have been ingrained in our brains that make us mediocre forever. AVERAGE… is the word most of us are aiming for.

Thankfully, I broke through it and I now have absolute clarity about money. If we leave our beliefs behind and open ourselves to new ideas, we can create magic the way I did in my life.

The first thing I did was that I believed in my abilities and did what I knew best - my clinical practice. Then I faced my fears and started working at dispelling them. Gratitude and the law of attraction worked for me. I started thinking that I have plenty of money to live in luxury. Every day, I visualized that all my loans are paid up.

I set my daily and long-term goals. And believe me, it works solid. People say that money can't buy you happiness. But I say "money is the source of all health and joy."

Yes, this statement is contrary to all the beliefs and morals of our cultured society. We have always been taught that don't be money minded. Don't be attracted to money. Money can't buy happiness… in my opinion, this is all nonsense!

If you don't have money, then you can't buy good health, good food, vacations, luxurious life, etc. You should always try to earn money and multiply it, of course, in legal and ethical ways. We are taught that study hard so that you can get a good job… that is also for money… right?

I also had this average/retrograde mindset, wherein I firmly believed that money can't buy happiness. But when I got submerged deeply into the lack of money and then fought my way back to riches, I realized that money is the root cause of all my joy and health.

Recently, one of my dentist friends called up.

"Hi Kunal, what's up man? I am entrapped in deep trouble!"

I understood the problem he was about to discuss with me. I answered, "I am doing fantastic. But you don't sound so encouraging?"

"Yeah," he replied sadly, "I have been trying to sail through covid these two years. I have somehow survived, but am buried under a pile of loans, and the practice is also not so good. I don't know what to do. I am just running behind money, but it's not coming to me. My health is also on the downside. I have developed diabetes."

I said, "My friend, you don't have to run behind money. Instead, it should be the other way round. Money should be attracted to you."

Friend: "Stop talking rubbish Kunal. I have tried everything and nothing works."

And he hung up.

I felt sorry for him. It was not him speaking, but his age-old beliefs and wrong conceptions about money.

Money is very emotional and touchy. We can also say it is a form of energy. Money comes to you if you are grateful for what you have. Every monetary transaction you do, you should be thankful for it. This gratitude for money is the real magnet. This is the secret I am giving to you because it worked well for me and it works every time for everyone.

You should have a feeling of abundance in your life. Feel that you have infinite money. Never ever live in your misery. The moment you start thinking about your lack of money and start dwelling on it, the universe starts giving you more lack of money.

You just have to demand, and the universe will give it to you. It's true for money as well. You can ask for any insane amount of money and if done properly, you will definitely get it.

Do you want to know what did I do apart from hard work to come out of my financial mess?

1. I stopped whining about the lack of money.

2. I started planning about the next luxury holiday I will be taking.

3. Every morning after meditation, I closed my eyes and imagined that I have received a huge sum of money. I felt the happiness of having so much money and how I would use it. On some days, tears of joy would spill from my eyes during this practice.

4. I started setting high goals.

5. I increased my efforts for a good life.

EXERCISE

1. Make a simple balance sheet. Take a page and divide it into two parts.

On the right side, enter your value - it may be the money you have, investments, property, etc.

On the left side, enter your liabilities - loans, etc.

2. Take another sheet and write your monthly expenses on the right side and incomes and investments on the left side.

   This sheet will tell you if you are on the positive or negative side of finances.

   The above two sheets will give you your current status in the world of money.

3. Now make a list of all the financial goals with a deadline.

4. Write the above list in affirmative… e.g. I have XYZ amount of money. And then imagine yourself having that kind of money. You should feel the joy of it.

Repeat step 4 every day till you achieve your goals.

All this combined with karma got me the perfect mindset and I attracted a lot of good fortune.

Not to mention that I always asked the universe for everything I needed, but I never asked any of my friends and family for money!

You can also get this titanium money mindset. Go through this chapter again, if needed. Pick up a few gems, apply them to your life and see the miracle happen before your eyes.

MONEY TIPS

1. 30% of your income should go into your investments. This way, you can save for retirement and build a

very good corpus for the future. You can invest in mutual funds, SIPs, FDs, government bonds, etc.

My personal favorite is SIP and mutual funds. This way, I can stay ahead of inflation.

Hack: the rate of return from your investment should be more than the inflation rate. Else, your money starts depreciating.

2. 50% of your income can be spent on your expenses, EMIs, daily needs, health, school fees, etc.

3. If any money is left after investments and expenses, then that can be spent on luxuries, or this too can be invested.

4. Develop an emergency fund. It is the sum of money that helps you sustain your current lifestyle for 6 to 12 months, even if you stop earning. This is the cushion or the safety net for you.

IF YOU RESPECT AND PROTECT YOUR MONEY,
MONEY WILL RESPECT AND PROTECT YOU.

EXERCISE

1. Go through this chapter and write down three takeaways and three things you could implement in your life.

2. Start implementing those things for the next 30 days with full devotion and trust.

3. Continue these habits even after 30 days for excellent results.

CHAPTER SEVENTEEN

MONEY STRATEGIES

*"Money is only a tool. It will take you wherever you wish,
but it will not replace you as the driver."*
—Ayn Rand

*Only buy something that you'd be perfectly happy to hold
if the market shuts down for ten years."*
—Warren Buffett

I have already mentioned a lot about the money mindset in chapter 16 Money Matters. In this chapter, I am going to give you some practical tips on money, which I did for myself and that helped me to lead a financially free life.

Money is your best friend, and when everyone leaves you, money is something that will help you. Even your last penny will work for you.

Keeping this in mind, I have set three major financial goals for you:

1. Financial security
2. Money growth
3. Future goals

If we arrange these three in place, our life becomes much easier. It needs a lot of planning and gradual hard work.

1. FINANCIAL SECURITY

CONTINGENCY FUND

First of all, you should have a cushion of emergency funds that you can use in case you lose your job/business. This amount should be able to sustain your current lifestyle for at least 12 months.

Contingency funds should be personal and also for your business/establishment. For example, I have two contingency funds: one for my personal survival the other for the survival of my clinic.

This contingency fund should not be touched for anything else other than emergency survival.

It should be parked in a safe investment tool like FDs or debt funds or whatever you think is secure. You may also consult your financial advisor.

HEALTH INSURANCE

You should have health insurance for your whole family. It's a must. Apart from health insurance, also keep some funds aside for health issues.

Make sure that your insurance covers critical illness, cancer and other things.

Try to buy a cashless insurance.

TERM PLAN

It is a very vital element. Always have a term plan as suggested by your financial advisor. Term plan looks like a waste of money but the comfort of cushion it gives to your family is unmatchable.

ACCIDENT AND DISABILITY INSURANCE

Always have one for you as you never know what can happen the next moment. There have been numerous instances where proper insurances have saved many lives and families.

This is to make you financially secure.

2. MONEY GROWTH AND MANAGEMENT

All the surplus income you have should be invested wisely, as it is your hard-earned money. You should evaluate any investment tool with the following two criteria:

    a. Returns should be more than the rate of inflation

    b. It should be easy and fast to redeem the money

One of the most popular methods of investment is mutual funds. It is one of the tools which gives high returns over a period of time.

If you are investing in mutual funds, invest for a long time, and don't look at market fluctuations.

Another tool is SIP. In this method, a fixed amount is deducted from your account for a long time every month. This money is invested by experienced fund managers in mutual funds. The growth over a period of 15-20 years is astounding.

SIPs operate on the power of compounding. You won't even realize when your money started growing. This is one of my favorite tools.

FDs and PPF are other forms of investments, but the rate of return is very less.

3. FUTURE GOALS

While investing, always keep an eye on your future goals. These goals may be anything like children's education, their wedding, vacation, or retirement fund.

I recommend to start planning for your retirement the day you start working. There are a lot of pension funds available in the market, but I am suggesting otherwise.

One strategy is to start a SIP with the purpose of a retirement fund. Let it grow till you retire and then withdraw the whole amount and re-invest in a MIP (monthly income plan).

This way, you will have a huge corpus that won't be touched by you and, at the same time, you will make a monthly income, which will help you lead a very good life in your golden years.

GOLDEN TIP: Cut your loans. Repay them at the earliest and try not to take any further loans.

Loans set you back by many years. Don't let anything set you back in life. Instead, create funds for every need. You don't need to have a very huge income to invest.

Investments can be made to grow even by investing Rs. 5000 a month.

The only thing you need is a disciplined mind.

Another tip: All wealthy people have multiple sources of income. Be it anything you can think of. So start working towards another source of income which may be your passion, as taught to me by my mentor, Dev Sir.

The moment you start working on your passion, money follows you. Many people don't realize this and learn it the hard way. But I am giving you all in this book. All thanks to my mentors.

Money does not buy you happiness, but lack of money certainly buys you misery."

—*Daniel Kahneman*

EXERCISE

1. Make a list of your financial goals.

2. Make a timeline for achieving your goals.

3. Make sure you achieve your goals in the timeframe you have set.

CHAPTER EIGHTEEN

THE EXCUSE MINDSET

"He that good for making excuses is seldom good for anything else."
—Benjamin Franklin

It is better to offer no excuse than a bad one."
—George Washington

Do you know that 1% of the world's population has 90% of the wealth?

Do you know that 90% of us have a mediocre mindset? This mass mediocrity is a pandemic. It is all the result of our mindset and the beliefs which have been instilled in us since our childhood.

What is the difference between the top 1% and the rest? Have they come from some other planet? Are they taught in a different way? Do they eat differently? Noooooo… they are all like us and from amongst us. Then why is this difference? It is because of only one thing, which is the mindset.

What is mindset? It is the way we think, the way we think about ourselves, others and life. Mindset is the way we look at our problems and solve them or surrender to them. Where does this mindset come from? It comes from within. It comes from an open mind, and it comes from acceptance. Mindset can be developed and used as a potent armory for success. Developing a mindset needs guidance and proper coaching. In this book, I have designed a few exercises and the 30 days challenge schedule in such a way that if followed, you will develop a steel mindset needed for all the success and happiness in life.

Do you believe that you are born to be average and live an average life OR are you happy with your average life? Our society, since ancient times, has programmed in our mind that the average is good and successful. How many times have you listened to this from your parents - study else you won't get a job? So the benchmark set here is that getting a job is very good, even if it will give you an average life.

The result of such thinking and mindset is that as we grow up, we develop the excuse mindset. We always find a fancy story for all of our failures or average results. My mentor, Dev, calls it a mediocre mindset disease!

Giving excuses for your failure is the quickest recipe for disaster in life. This is because, if we keep on giving excuses, we never understand our mistakes, and then never learn from them to improve ourselves. If we don't enrich ourselves on a regular basis, it leads our brain cells to sit idle and gradually degenerate.

I have seen many people working at very high positions

in the corporate world or administration. They keep on blaming others for everything that happens to them and in their organization.

Or you might have come across people who are always late for all their appointments, and then their excuse is always ready... traffic or illness or some strange reason.

To live a life of health and wellness, and to transform your life in 30 days, you have to rise above the average mentality and stop hurling excuses. Great leaders and successful people always take responsibility and never shy away from seeing their mistakes, and they keep learning every day. Always remember that, however learned we are, there is always something new to learn. And you don't know in which form your teacher will come to you. You just have to develop an open and steel mindset, and the universe will raise your levels to such heights that no success will be away from you.

I call this excuse mindset as ostrich behavior. Have you seen an ostrich? It hides its face in its own body and thinks that the enemy won't see him. We do the same when we give an excuse. We fool ourselves and provide entertainment for onlookers.

When we start having an excuse mindset, the following sentences can be heard:

- Life is too bad... don't know what to do.
- Why is it me always?
- Nature is conspiring against me.
- My bad luck.
- Luck never seems to shine on me.

- Why do I have to always lose?
- It was not my fault. They favored the undeserving person!

Have you ever used these phrases? If yes, then my friend, you are in the majority of excuse givers!

These excuse givers are the mediocre people who are always happy in average lives.

They don't know what lies beyond the ordinary. That's where the success lies. We rise above average only after we stop giving excuses and move into the unknown.

There is so much to discover we do not even know exists. We just have to stop giving excuses to get that magical life.

Always remember that whatever happens to us, only and only we are to be blamed for it. Somewhere, we have plotted our own destiny.

Universe just listens to us and creates what we have asked for (the law of attraction). So we have to be careful in what we ask for ourselves.

Any promotion in a job or failure is always the culmination of our own actions and their results.

This holds true for any result; positive or negative. To fetch good results, we have to work very hard. That is our action. This action ultimately translates into a RESULT.

If we don't work hard, that's also an action-giving negative result.

We have to decide whether we want to be on the negative side by giving excuses or on the winning side by taking responsibility for our actions.

Always remember, no one other than our own selves are responsible for whatever happens to us.

"The only thing standing between you and your goal is the bullshit story you keep telling yourself as to why you can't achieve it."

—Jordan Belfort

EXERCISE

1. Sit down peacefully in a place where no one will disturb you for 10 minutes. Now make a list of all the times when you have ever made excuses and blamed others for your fault.

2. Read the list carefully and pledge not to repeat those. Instead, face it and win like a warrior.

CHAPTER NINETEEN

MIND MAP

Here is a simple template to follow every morning, which can help your mind grow.

I have explained each of these steps in detail in the chapters on mental health. Follow these steps religiously every day, and you will see that you have become a new, calmer and wonderful human being.

CHAPTER TWENTY
MONEY MAP

By now, it is well understood that money is an important pillar of life and we can't ignore or demonize it.

Here is a road map to money that will definitely help you secure your future.

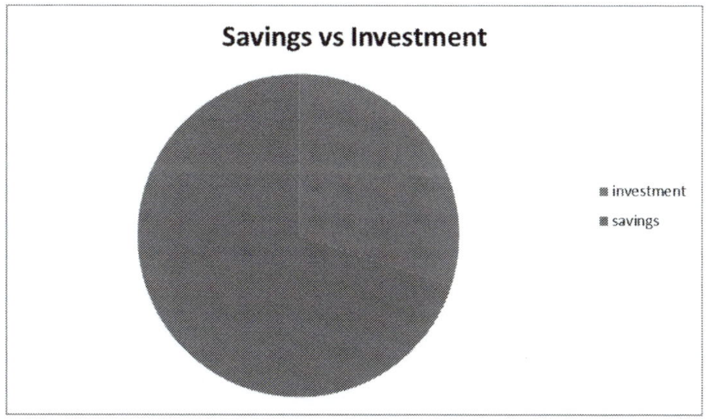

As also mentioned earlier, every month, you should invest 30% of your savings.

Savings are needed for your financial health. The earlier you start saving, the better it is. I have explained about savings in the chapter 16 Money Matters.

Take a paper and pen and write down all the loans you have.

Calculate the total amount due and chalk out a plan to pay it off by a pre-set date. The sooner you pay off your loans, the more you are in control of your life.

CHAPTER TWENTY ONE
ROAD MAP

By now, I am sure you have understood the concepts I have explained in this book. You also know my story, struggles, and how I overcame them. I do not have an iota of doubt that now you are raring to go and GIVE IT ALL towards a magical life.

I have made a roadmap for you, that is simple to follow. You can make slight changes to it according to your engagements.

This is a generic road map that is suggested for improving your life. But it's you who knows your true situation like health, medical conditions, etc. so follow the steps in accordance with your medical condition.

Activity	*Suggested Time*	*Outcome*
Wake up	5 am	Extra me-time
Gratitude	5 am	Sets the tone for the day

Activity	Suggested Time	Outcome
Meditate/Visualize/ Read	5:15 to 5:30 am	Mental peace, knowledge, call to the universe
Exercise	6-7 am	Physical fitness and happy hormones
Family time	7-9 am	Relations
Day planning	9 am	Prioritize
Intense work	9-12 pm	Get the maximum out of your day
Relaxed work	12 pm to 4 pm	Less important work done
Back home	5 pm	Relax
Exercise/walk	30 mins	Revs up metabolism* suggested by The 5 AM Club, Robin Sharma
Dinner	7 pm to 7:30 pm	Early dinner is good for health
Bedtime	9 pm	Early to bed

This road map, if followed holistically, gives you adequate time for work, play and rest. You also have adequate family time.

This chart is based on my 8*3 formula. Refer to the chapter The 8*3 Formula.

CONCLUSION

I am sure by now you are feeling overwhelmed by all the information. I can understand.

I was in the same position for years when I started learning from various sources. It took me 15 years to discover all the knowledge. Many mentors taught me and I had to make a lot of investment in terms of time and money. I have condensed all this knowledge into the form of this book.

I wish I had such guidance when I was learning. So, use this book as a key and shortcut to a very good and magical life. If you go through the text carefully, you may find the purpose of your life and all the success you ever dreamed of.

I have implemented all the concepts and methods on myself and these have proven to be highly successful for me and my mentees. Trust these techniques and concepts, and you will open a floodgate of goodness in your life.

I have shared exercises at the end of most chapters. Do these exercises with accountability and you will be able to squeeze the maximum out of this book.

If you are still wondering where to start, I suggest rereading it chapter by chapter and doing the exercises one by one. I advocate reading this book in around 3-4 days the first time. During the second read, you can start doing the exercises.

I am sure reading this book has been a good investment of time for you. It took me around a year to finish and refine this book. I understand that however good a book is, nothing can be better than me and my team helping you and working closely with you on your magical life.

If you intend to learn more and work more closely with me, I invite you to one of our magical life events. You can join our community on Facebook and Instagram:

https://www.facebook.com/groups/353390826884196

https://instagram.com/drkunalbankalifestylecoach

And please leave a message for us after you apply. Someone from our team will get in touch with you for further association.

If you are a good fit, will get a chance to work closely with me under the mentorship program.

I want you to dig deeper and achieve bigger.

Thanks for spending your time with me.

Dr. Kunal Banka

PS: Give It All!

SUGGESTED READS

1. 6 Sundays A Week Life by Dev Gadhvi

2. 80%Mindset 20%Skills by Dev Gadhvi

3. The Magic by Rhonda Byrne

4. The Secret by Rhonda Byrne

5. The 10x Rule by Grant Cardone

6. Can't hurt me by David Goggins

7. Crush It by Gary Vaynerchuk

8. The 5 AM Club by Robin Sharma

9. Atomic Habits by James Clear

10. Odyssey series by Arthur C. Clarke

These are just a few to begin with. There are many more books to be read. So, keep adding to the list.

ACKNOWLEDGMENT

It was a long journey on the way to the completion of this book. There were so many people who helped me actualize the manuscript.

First and foremost, I would like to thank the two most important ladies of my life, my daughter Iris and wife Juhi. They have endured long hours of my absence when I was busy writing.

Juhi has always been my most harsh critic and I thank her for this, as without her constructive criticism, this book and my life would not have been perfect.

My parents are always a pillar of strength for me. My father, Mr. Ashok Banka, always listened to me carefully, even when my ideas were not very appealing. His insight has been the elixir of this book. I always look up to him in all my endeavors. One small word of encouragement from him always boosted my writing and research for the book.

My mother, Mrs. Geetanjali, has been clinical in providing the right motivation for me whenever I was down. It was for her that I decided to pen this book.

I have always learned from my younger brother, Kanishq, who is an acclaimed writer himself. I am grateful to my family members for providing the right environment and support.

I have been lucky to have the finest gurus in my life. My Guru, Dev Gadhvi, has been instrumental in mentoring me and no amount of thanks can be enough. My co-mentors, Mrs. Anju Chowdhary and Mr. Manoj Sharma, have been meticulous in guiding me through all the ups and downs.

Dr. Rajiv Verma has been influential in transforming my personal and professional life through the years and I will be always grateful to you, sir.

Thanks to all my teachers who have shaped my life so wonderfully.

Special gratitude to Dr. Nitin Kulkarni (IAS) and Mrs. Suman Gupta (IPS) for always guiding me and encouraging me. Thanks for being there.

I am grateful to my best friend Dr. Keerti Shetty Vittal (DDS) for always helping me out whenever I hit a wall.

Extreme gratitude to the universe for getting the right things at the right time for me.

Thank you, thank you, thank you!